Leaders

The Life of God in the
Soul of Man

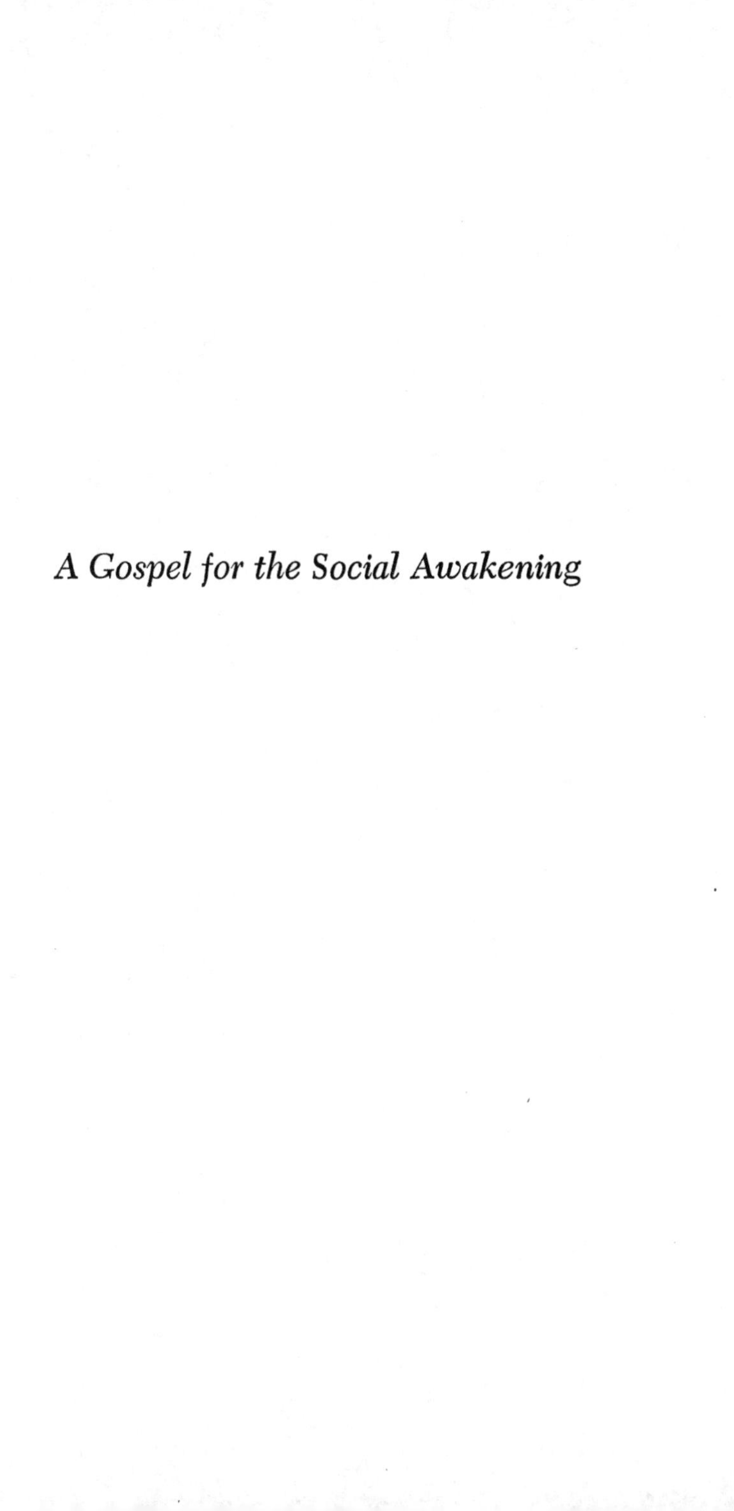

A Gospel for the Social Awakening

A Gospel *for the* Social Awakening

SELECTIONS FROM THE WRITINGS OF

Walter Rauschenbusch

---

compiled by
BENJAMIN E. MAYS
with an introduction by
C. HOWARD HOPKINS

WIPF & STOCK · Eugene, Oregon

Wipf and Stock Publishers
199 W 8th Ave, Suite 3
Eugene, OR 97401

A Gospel for the Social Awakening
Selections from the Writings of Walter Rauschenbusch
By Rauschenbusch, Walter
ISBN 13: 978-1-60608-034-4
Publication date 7/2/2008
Previously published by Haddam House, 1950

Acknowledgments

Grateful acknowledgment is made to The Macmillan Company for permission to use selections from *Christianizing the Social Order* and *A Theology for the Social Gospel*; to The Pilgrim Press for selections from *Prayers of the Social Awakening* and *Unto Me*; to the Estate of Walter Rauschenbusch for selections from *Christianity and the Social Crisis* and *The Social Principles of Jesus*.

Sources

Christianity and the Social Crisis, The Macmillan Company, New York, 1920

Christianizing the Social Order, The Macmillan Company, New York, 1912

Prayers of the Social Awakening, The Pilgrim Press, Boston, 1910

The Social Principles of Jesus, Association Press, New York, 1916

A Theology for the Social Gospel, The Macmillan Company, New York, 1918

Unto Me, The Pilgrim Press, Boston, 1912

"The New Evangelism," *The Independent,* New York, May 12, 1904

Foreword

If a poll were taken among informed Christians on the question "Who are our twentieth century prophets?" it is almost certain that the name of Walter Rauschenbusch would be high on the list. Many persons now in or past middle age will testify that the writings of Rauschenbusch were an important formative influence in their youth. College students, particularly in the first decades of this century, were inspired by *The Social Principles of Jesus* and *Prayers of the Social Awakening*. Young ministers were stirred by the ringing challenge of a man who combined an Old Testament cry for social justice with a New Testament emphasis on love and forgiveness.

Yet even the most forceful message grows dim with the passing of the years and even the best sellers of one generation are soon forgotten when they are out of print. The realization that many young people today never heard of Walter Rauschenbusch and never read a paragraph of his pioneering works led the Editorial

Board of Haddam House to seek a manuscript that would make the best of Rauschenbusch available to present-day readers.

An invitation to compile this anthology was extended to Dr. Benjamin E. Mays, President of Morehouse College, and willingly accepted. As an educator in the deep South and as an international leader of young people, Dr. Mays has reflected the convictions which motivated Walter Rauschenbusch and is in this generation a prophet of the gospel for a social awakening.

It was decided that the thoughts of Rauschenbusch should be presented not as a series of book digests but in a sequence of chapters organized around his major emphases. It has been felt advisable to select those passages from Rauschenbusch's voluminous writings which are most pertinent to our day. Dr. Mays is responsible for the selection and for most of the chapter titles and subheadings.

The Board felt that an introductory chapter would add greatly to the value of this anthology by providing the biographical background and social setting in which the prophetic message of Walter Rauschenbusch could be more fully appreciated. For this interpretation they turned to Dr. C. Howard Hopkins, whose *The Rise of the Social Gospel in American Protestantism* is a definitive study in this field of church history. Readers will agree that Dr. Hopkins has presented just enough historical data to enable them to approach the writings of Rauschenbusch with anticipation and understanding.

The social and theological climate since the days of

Foreword

Walter Rauschenbusch has changed perceptibly. Some of the assumptions underlying the social gospel have been questioned sharply. Some of the specific issues which concerned Rauschenbusch and his contemporaries are no longer points of controversy; the battle has moved on to new fronts. Even the term "social gospel" in some quarters carries a connotation of unwarranted optimism and one-sided emphasis. But the pendulum of criticism has a tendency to swing too far and to rely too much on second-hand sources. One who reads Rauschenbusch for the first time at midcentury is likely still to sense across the years a note of vitality and prophetic insight. One who rereads Rauschenbusch, even though his faith in social awakening may be somewhat dimmed by two wars and a depression, is likely to realize that this man was too profound in his interpretation of the Christian gospel to be outdated and and that the awakening for which he longed is overdue. Truly this man has something to say to our times.

PAUL M. LIMBERT.

Contents

An American Prophet

A Biographical Sketch of Walter Rauschenbusch

by C. HOWARD HOPKINS

Walter Rauschenbusch, like an Old Testament prophet, was possessed by the compulsive power of a great idea, an idea that to him reflected the very heart of Jesus' teaching and the purpose of his life and death. His proclamation of this "new revelation" impressed his generation so deeply that it became a classic American formulation of Christian ethics. Much of what he said is as valid for us as it was for our parents. A seasoned European traveler, Rauschenbusch once wrote:

In the Alps I have seen the summit of some great mountain come out of the clouds in the early morning and stand revealed in blazing purity. Its foot was still swathed in drifting mist, but I knew the mountain was there and my soul rejoiced in it. So Christ's conception of the Kingdom of God came to me as a new revelation. Here was the idea and purpose that had dominated the mind of the Master himself. All his teachings center about it. His life was given to it. His death was suffered for it. When a man has once seen that in the gospels, he can never unsee it again.

The result was that the *Cambridge History of American Literature* characterized Rauschenbusch as "perhaps the most creative spirit in the American theological world." How was it that he received his revelation and what did it comprise?

Born in Rochester, New York, in 1861, where he spent his life save for ten years in New York City and several interludes of study abroad, one of Rauschenbusch's earliest memories was of draping the front door with crepe for Lincoln's funeral. He died in 1918, when the nation was again engaged in titanic struggle. Thus Rauschenbusch's life spanned the dynamic half century of America's conversion from the rural simplicity that Lincoln had known to the urban and industrial complexity of the twentieth century. Educated in his home town and in Europe, young Rauschenbusch, whose Baptist heritage was engrafted upon a family tree rooted in six generations of Lutheran ministers, planned on a foreign missionary career. But there was some flaw in his orthodoxy and the appointment was canceled. Instead he chose the tough assignment offered by a struggling German Baptist church in West Forty-fifth Street, Manhattan, at a salary of six hundred dollars a year.

Eleven years among the laboring people living in the very shadows of the world's greatest wealth yet "out of work, out of clothes, out of shoes, and out of hope" found the young pastor's deeply spiritual but highly individualistic ethics inadequate to the needs of the endless procession of needy men and women who "wore down our threshold and wore away our hearts." In his desire to serve his flock young Rauschenbusch arose too soon from a sickbed and incurred a relapse that cost him his hearing. This intensified his concern to find a way to lift the load of those with whom he lived all week and preached to on Sundays.

These strenuous years were the formative experience of Rauschenbusch's life. Numerous influences converged upon his sensitive conscience. A friend has described some of them:

> Henry George and Bellamy and Mazzini and Karl Marx and Tolstoi influenced him some, but above all the crying need of the comfortless multitude and the senseless inadequacy of competitive strife, the apparent possibility of co-operative service and the jubilant remedy of the message of the Kingdom took hold of his susceptible soul.

Henry George, whom every student of American life knows as a militant crusader for righteousness and social justice through the "single tax" and who made a good run for the mayoralty of New York, first awakened Rauschenbusch's mind through his provocative tract, *Progress and Poverty*. Edward Bellamy's utopian novel, *Looking Backward, 2000–1887*, has the familiarity of required reading in American history, but to young Rauschenbusch and thousands like him it came as a powerful call to reform. In 1891 he had a year of study in Germany, devoting himself to sociology and the teachings of Jesus, which he thought "a good combination and likely to produce results." He visited British co-operatives en route and was so impressed that he planned to write a book about them.

Another influence in shaping Rauschenbusch's mind was a cell group that he and a few other young ministers started in order "to realize the ethical and spiritual principles of Jesus, both in their individual and social aspects." One of them suggested that the organization be devoted to "the study and realization" of the idea of the Kingdom of God, so the name "Brotherhood of the Kingdom" was adopted. For more than twenty years it met every summer for a week's discussion of what came to be called the social gospel. The members pledged themselves to "exemplify obedience to the ethics of Jesus" in their personal lives and to "propagate the thoughts of Jesus" to the limits of their ability. They were to "lay stress on the social aims of Christianity" while endeavoring to make "Christ's teaching concerning wealth operative in the Church." Expected to "take pains to keep in touch with the common people," the brothers pledged themselves to try "to infuse the religious spirit into the efforts for social amelioration." These practical aims resulted in considerable influence not only upon members of the group, who had few illusions about the odds they were facing, but affected the social gospel movement noticeably. The frank give-and-take of the Brotherhood served as an anvil upon which Rauschenbusch's thought was hammered out. "Only where mind touches mind, does the mind do its best work," he once wrote in the guest book at the conference home.

Together with a few friends Rauschenbusch attempted to publish a paper in 1889–91, devoted to "the interests of the working people of New York City." Called *For the Right*, the little sheet tackled the giants of greed, monopoly, maldistribution, and the condition of labor, "from the standpoint of Christian-Socialism." Greeted by the *Times* as "radical yet Christian," it boldly declared what it thought "every pulpit in New York ought to be saying." Through it Rauschenbusch endorsed the eight-hour day and advocated municipal ownership of the new subway. He declared that "surely there must be a hitch somewhere" in a system in which maldistribution gave a few people "as nice furniture or as many clothes" as they wanted or as "the women folks would like to have," although the earth abounded in "any quantity of material" that could be dug out of it and there were "thousands of skillful hands only too eager to work this raw material up into all the shapes that would be useful to mankind." Yet help could not be expected from the rich and educated: it must come through the workers themselves. *For the Right* went the way of all such papers—only two files of it can be found—but Rauschenbusch was neither discouraged nor embittered because reform was slow. In fact, one of the reasons why he ultimately made such a mark on his times was that he was not baffled by the twentieth century as were some of his contemporaries such as Mark Twain or Henry Adams. Because of a faith which they lacked, he could see the slow-moving purpose of God at work in human society.

In accepting the religious ideas of his time, Rauschenbusch was naturally a product of the day in which he lived. There were of course theological conservatives and radicals as well as liberals in American Protestantism in the latter years of the nineteenth century. Rauschenbusch's own background was conservative and he was set back on his heels when the ethics of his traditionally pietistic faith failed to answer the cry of the working class among whom he labored in New York's "Hell's Kitchen." In constructing a new formulation of Christian ethics, Rauschenbusch remained solidly anchored to the great affirmations of Hebrew-Christian faith—the existence of God and his activity in human history, the expression of his grace through Jesus Christ, and the hope of salvation for mankind.

At the time Rauschenbusch was developing his philosophy, Americans were much concerned about the effect of Darwinian evolution upon religious ideas. Conservatives rejected evolution and radicals threw out most of Christianity. Between these extremes a group of able thinkers found what seemed to them an enrichment of Christian thought through the new insights. Washington Gladden, an older contemporary of Rauschenbusch, set forth this viewpoint in a small book of sermons published in 1896 entitled *Ruling Ideas of the Present Age*. He held (1) that evolution had given meaning to the idea of the indwelling of God in man, or the doctrine of immanence. Although this conception had been given prominence by Spinoza, for the "progressive" theologians of this period—as they called themselves some years before the politicians fell upon the word—it meant that the transcendent God of Christianity could be seen at work in the processes of human society as well as in the larger universe. God, said Rauschenbusch, is "the common basis of all our life." Another "ruling idea" was (2) that society is better described by the analogy to an organism than any other way. Indebted to Herbert Spencer at this point, these men thought of human interrelationships as "vital and organic" rather than scattered like grains of sand. Rauschenbusch preferred the word "solidaristic." St. Paul's comparison of the Church to the human body represents the "highest possible philosophy of human society." When one man sins, others suffer; when one social class sins, others are involved. Consciousness of solidarity is a fundamental component of an ethical and social religion. "We love and serve God when we love and serve our fellows, whom he loves and in whom he lives," he wrote.

For Rauschenbusch as for many of his colleagues, these stimulating new ideas were structured in (3) the concept of the Kingdom of God, which we have seen burst upon him like the dawn. The Kingdom brought both the newer ways of thinking and the unanswered social and ethical questions into focus. In his mind, the Kingdom was a universal ideal that included the entire social existence of humanity: it is the whole of the social gospel, he once exclaimed. To the explanation and application of this idea he gave much of his best thought. It was the sum of his philosophy of life and of his religion, as the selections from his writing in this book make clear.

From the viewpoint of the infinitely more tragic world of 1950 the hopefully progressive theology of the pre-World War I years seems a bit naive. This criticism is legitimate, especially when leveled against Rauschenbusch's fellows, but it is hardly so if raised concerning him. In reading his writings today it must be borne in mind that Rauschenbusch was exerting his every energy to awaken the Church, to awaken Christians to their social duty as citizens, as members of the human race, as Americans living in a mutually interdependent society. He took for granted that his readers held a fairly generally accepted body of inherited religious ideas. He was concerned to moralize these, to domesticate them in the twentieth century, to bring God into reality as an active force for good in human affairs. Thus he seems sometimes to have been a "mere moralist." He was indeed a Christian moralist, but not a mere moralist; his thought hinged on God, not upon ethics; his Kingdom was the Kingdom of God that included man, not simply the kingdom of man.

In 1897 Rauschenbusch was called to his home city to teach in the German department of the Rochester Theological Seminary. As a teacher—first of New Testament, natural science, and civil government—he now read even more widely than had been his habit in the pastorate. (The little church had, by the way, grown and moved to a more strategic location; on the tenth anniversary of Rauschenbusch's ministry many letters had been received from distinguished people, but the butcher who spoke for the congregation remarked simply that they had found in their pastor "more that is Christlike than in any human being we have ever met.") Five years after taking over this sizable teaching assignment, Rauschenbusch was asked to fill the chair of Church History in the English division of the Seminary. This he held through the rest of his life. In Rochester he at once allied himself with progressive elements and so entered into civic life that at his death it was said that the city had lost its "first citizen." As he studied, taught, preached, and meditated upon the history of Christianity, the message that had been conceived during the stormy years of his "Hell's Kitchen" pastorate began to come to birth.

Although Rauschenbusch had been fairly prolific as a writer of magazine articles and was well known in Baptist circles, his first book, *Christianity and the Social Crisis,* established him at once as the leader of the social gospel movement upon its publication in 1907. No one was more surprised than he to return from Europe to find himself banqueted at a swank New York hotel and called upon for speeches the nation over. Written in two vacation periods of six weeks each, the book contrasted the social power of the early Christian Church with its present impotence and gave a practical turn to the discussion by suggesting in a final chapter "what to do." In 1910 there came from his pen but more deeply from his heart one of the most unique books any American religious writer has produced—a small volume of prayers entitled *For God and the People*. Reprinted as *Prayers of the Social Awakening*, it remains forty years afterward virtually the only literature of its kind. Two years later his second argument, *Christianizing the Social Order*, came from the press. "Wholly without a note of hatred," it was a careful analysis of "our semi-Christian social order" from the frankly socialistic viewpoint. In 1916 he wrote a popular study manual on *The Social Principles of Jesus*, which was widely distributed among the armed forces in World War I, giving it the largest circulation of any of his works. The last and perhaps the greatest of Rauschenbusch's books was written for a smaller audience. Originally presented as the Taylor Lectures at the Yale Divinity School in 1917, almost at the moment America was declaring war on Germany, *A Theology for the Social Gospel* contained his ripened thought, in which the idea of the Kingdom of God was again central. Selections from all of these books have been included in this anthology.

Rauschenbusch's criticism of capitalism was essentially that of Fabian socialism, as seen by a religious-minded student deeply concerned with human values. A social order that "tempts, defeats, drains, and degrades, and leaves men stunted, cowed, and shamed in their manhood" can make no claim to being Christian, he insisted. Competition ("the law of tooth and nail"), the monopolistic and dictatorial nature of corporations, business dishonesty, the profit motive—these came under his strictures. In contrast and in opposition to these features of the American scene, Rauschenbusch pointed to several areas which he believed had been to some extent "Christianized"—the family, the Church, agencies of education, and political life as far as it had been genuinely democratized. As he saw them, the requisites of a "Christian" order were social justice—most important and underlying all others—collective property rights, industrial democracy, reasonable equality, and co-operation. Social change was for the "unsaved" institutions, chiefly economic life, to be brought under the law of Christ, which meant into conformity with these principles. If this seems overly simple, let us recall that Rauschenbusch's life was spent in the years before World War I; that he was a prophet rather than a politician or social planner; that his gospel was "the old message of salvation, but enlarged and intensified."

More than one audience that heard Rauschenbusch felt itself "listening in a way to a prophet," as a newspaper commented. To ask what he would counsel today about the divorce rate, the H-bomb, bacterial warfare, the indifference of the Church, alcoholism and the traffic menace, heart disease, communism, or the abuse of power by labor—which he trusted to bring about social improvement—is to ask what an Old Testament prophet combined of Amos and Hosea would advise. "My sole desire," he declared, "has been to summon the Christian passion for justice and the Christian powers of love and mercy to do their share in redeeming our social order from its inherent wrongs."

Rauschenbusch's realization that social problems stem from the "inherent wrongs" of the social order gives his writing permanent relevance. Many of his colleagues assumed that the ills of society could be cured by legislating piecemeal reforms. Rauschenbusch thought this was useful but he saw that a realistic program for social change must deal with the root causes of social maladjustment and that it must be politically effectual. He understood that pleas for charity, stewardship, or even for justice would go unheeded in a world of pressure groups and power politics unless they were supported by the votes and pressures of those concerned. Hence his gospel went beyond the sermon to the ballot box. In reading him we may gain some insight as to this necessity but more significantly share his vision of the redemptive power of the Kingdom of God—an irresistible ideal set against and above the stubborn actualities of politics, poverty, or pressures.

A Gospel for the Social Awakening

A Challenge to Youth

This matter of raising the moral standards of society is preeminently an affair of the young. They must do it or it will never be done. The Sermon on the Mount was spoken by a young man, and it moves with the impetuous virility of youth. . . . While we are young is the time to make a forward run with the flag of Christ, the banner of justice and love, and plant it on the heights yonder. We must not only be better men and women than we are now. We must leave a better world behind us when we are through with it. Whatever we affirm in our growing years will work out in some fashion in our years of maturity and power. If fifty thousand college men and women a year would range themselves alongside of Jesus Christ, look at our present world as open-eyed as he looked at his world, see where the social standards of conduct are in contradiction with his spirit and with modern need, and work to raise them, the world would feel the effect in ten years. And those who strive in that way would live by faith in the higher commonwealth of God and have some of its nobility of spirit.

—Walter Rauschenbusch,
[*The Social Principles of Jesus*, p. 92.]

1

The Christian Gospel and Our Social Crisis

THE CRY OF CRISIS!

The cry of "Crisis! crisis!" has become a weariness. Every age and every year are critical and fraught with destiny. Yet in the widest survey of history Western civilization is now at a decisive point in its development.

Will some Gibbon of Mongol race sit by the shore of the Pacific in the year A.D. 3000 and write on the "Decline and Fall of the Christian Empire"? If so, he will probably describe the nineteenth and twentieth centuries as the golden age when outwardly life flourished as never before, but when that decay, which resulted in the gradual collapse of the twenty-first and twenty-second centuries, was already far advanced.

Or will the twentieth century mark for the future historian the real adolescence of humanity, the great emancipation from barbarism and from the paralysis of injustice, and the beginning of a progress in the intellectual, social, and moral life of mankind to which all past history has no parallel?

It will depend almost wholly on the moral forces which the Christian nations can bring to the fighting line against wrong, and the fighting energy of those moral forces will again depend on the degree to which they are inspired by religious faith and enthusiasm. It is either a revival of social religion or the deluge.

WHY NATIONS DECAY

Nations do not die by wealth, but by injustice. The forward impetus comes through some great historical opportunity which stimulates the production of wealth, breaks up the caked and rigid order of the past, sets free the energies of new classes, calls creative leaders to the front, quickens the intellectual life, intensifies the sense of duty and the ideal devotion to the common weal, and awakens in the strong individuals the large ambition of patriotic service. Progress slackens when a single class appropriates the social results of the common labor, fortifies its evil rights by unfair laws, throttles the masses by political centralization and suppression, and consumes in luxury what it has taken in covetousness. Then there is a gradual loss of productive energy, an increasing bitterness and distrust, a waning sense of duty and devotion to country, a paralysis of the moral springs of noble action. Men no longer love the Commonwealth, because it does not stand for the common wealth. Force has to supply the cohesive power which love fails to furnish. Exploitation creates poverty, and poverty is followed by physical degeneration. Education, art, wealth, and culture may continue to advance and may even ripen to their mellowest perfection when the worm of death is already at the heart of the nation. Internal convulsions or external catastrophes will finally reveal the state of decay.

It is always a process extending through generations or even centuries. It is possible that with the closely knit nations of the present era the resistive vitality is greater than in former ages, and it will take much longer for them to break up. The mobility of modern intellectual life will make it harder for the stagnation of mind and the crystallization of institutions to make headway. But unless the causes of social wrong are removed, it will be a slow process of strangulation and asphyxiation.

In the last resort the only hope is in the moral forces which can be summoned to the rescue. If there are statesmen, prophets, and apostles who set truth and justice above selfish advancement; if their call finds a response in the great body of the people; if a new tide of religious faith and moral enthusiasm creates new standards of duty and a new capacity for self-sacrifice; if the strong learn to direct their love of power to the uplifting of the people and see the highest self-assertion in self-sacrifice—then the intrenchments of vested wrong will melt away; the stifled energy of the people will leap forward; the atrophied members of the social body will be filled with a fresh flow of blood; and a regenerate nation will look with the eyes of youth across the fields of the future.

OUR COLLECTIVE SINS

Men used to feel acute guilt if they had committed some ritual oversight, such as touching a taboo thing, eating meat on Friday, or working on the Sabbath. The better teachings of modern Christianity and general religious indifference have combined to reduce that sort of fear and guilt.

On the other hand we are becoming much more sensitive about collective sins in which we are involved. I have a neighbor who owns stock in a New England cotton mill. Recently the company opened a factory in North Carolina and began to employ child labor. This man's young daughter faded away when she was emerging from childhood, and so he thinks of the other girls, who are breathing cotton fluff for him. A correspondent wrote me whose husband, a man of national reputation, had bought stock in a great steel company. She is a Jewess and a pacifist. When the plant began to devote itself to the manufacture of shrapnel and bombs . . . she felt involved. But what was her husband to do with the stock? Would it make things better if he passed the war-stained property to another man? I know a woman whose father, back in the nineties, took a fortune out of a certain dirty mill town. She is now living on his fortune; but the children of the mill-hands are living on their misfortune. No effort of hers can undo more than a fraction of the evil which was set in motion while that fortune was being accumulated.

If these burdens of conscience were foolish or morbid, increased insight and a purer Christian teaching would lift them. But it is increased insight and Christian feeling which created them. An unawakened person does not inquire on whose life juices his big dividends are fattening. Upper-class minds have been able to live parasitic lives without any fellow-feeling for the peasants or tenants whom they were draining to pay for their leisure. Modern democracy brings these lower fellow-men up to our field of vision. Then if man has drawn any real religious feeling from Christ, his participation in the systematized oppression of civilization will, at least at times, seem an intolerable burden and guilt. Is this morbid? Or is it morbid to live on without such realization? Those who today are still without a consciousness of collective wrong must be classified as men of darkened mind.

WHAT IS THE SOCIAL GOSPEL?

The social gospel is the old message of salvation, but enlarged and intensified. The individualistic gospel has taught us to see the sinfulness of every human heart and has inspired us with faith in the willingness and power of God to save every soul that comes to him. But it has not given us an adequate understanding of the sinfulness of the social order and its share in the sins of all individuals within it. It has not evoked faith in the will and power of God to redeem the permanent institutions of human society from their inherited guilt of oppression and extortion. Both our sense of sin and our faith in salvation have fallen short of the realities under its teaching. The social gospel seeks to bring men under repentance for their collective sins and to create a more sensitive and more modern conscience. It calls on us for the faith of the old prophets who believed in the salvation of nations.

The adjustment of the Christian message to the regeneration of the social order is plainly one of the most difficult tasks ever laid on the intellect of religious leaders. The pioneers of the social gospel have had a hard time trying to consolidate their old faith and their new aim. Some have lost their faith; others have come out of the struggle with crippled formulations of truth. Does not our traditional theology deserve some of the blame for this spiritual wastage because it left these men without spiritual support and allowed them to become the vicarious victims of our theological inefficiency? If our theology is silent on social salvation, we compel college men and women, workingmen, and thelogical students to choose between an unsocial system of theology and an irreligious system of social salvation. It is not hard to predict the outcome. If we seek to keep Christian doctrine unchanged, we shall ensure its abandonment.

Instead of being an aid in the development of the social gospel, systematic theology has often been a real clog. When a minister speaks to his people about child labor or the exploitation of the lowly by the strong; when he insists on adequate food, education, recreation, and a really human opportunity for all, there is response. People are moved by plain human feeling and by the instinctive convictions which they have learned from Jesus Christ. But at once there are doubting and dissenting voices. We are told that environment has no saving power; regeneration is what men need; we cannot have a regenerate society without regenerate individuals; we do not live for this world but for the life to come; it is not the function of the Church to deal with economic questions; any effort to change the social order before the coming of the Lord is foredoomed to failure. These objections all issue from the theological consciousness created by traditional church teaching. These half-truths are the proper product of a halfway system of theology in which there is no room for social redemption. Thus the Church is halting between two voices that call it. On the one side is the voice of the living Christ amid living men today; on the other side is the voice of past ages embodied in theology. Who will say that the authority of this voice has never confused our Christian judgment and paralyzed our determination to establish God's kingdom on earth?

The social gospel calls for an expansion in the scope of salvation and for more religious dynamic to do the work of God. It requires more faith and not less. It offers a more thorough and durable salvation. It is able to create a more searching sense of sin and to preach repentance to the respectable and mighty who have ridden humanity to the mouth of hell.

Power in religion comes only through the consciousness of a great elementary need which compels men to lay hold of God anew. The social gospel speaks to such a need, and where a real harmony has been established it has put new fire and power into the old faith.

THEOLOGY SHOULD BE CREATIVE

The great religious thinkers who created theology were always leaders who were shaping ideas to meet actual situations. The new theology of Paul was a product of fresh religious experience and of practical necessities. His idea that the Jewish law had been abrogated by Christ's death was worked out in order to set his mission to the Gentiles free from the crippling grip of the past and to make an international religion of Christianity. Luther worked out the doctrine of "justification by faith" because he had found by experience that it gave him a surer and happier way to God than the effort to win merit by his own works. But that doctrine became the foundation of a new theology for whole nations because it proved to be the battle cry of a great social and religious upheaval and the effective means of breaking down the semipolitical power of the clergy, of shutting up monasteries, of secularizing church property, and of increasing the economic and political power of city councils and princes. There is nothing else in sight today which has power to rejuvenate theology except the consciousness of vast sins and sufferings, and the longing for righteousness and a new life, which are expressed in the social gospel.

THE SOCIAL GOSPEL IS NOT NEW

The social gospel is, in fact, the oldest gospel of all. It is built on the foundation of the apostles and prophets. Its substance is the Hebrew faith which Jesus himself held. If the prophets ever talked about the plan of redemption, they meant the social redemption of the nation. So long as John the Baptist and Jesus were proclaiming the gospel, the Kingdom of God was its central word, and the ethical teaching of both, which was their practical commentary and definition of the Kingdom idea, looked toward a higher social order in which the new ethical standards would become practicable. To the first generation of disciples the hope of the Lord's return meant the hope of a Christian social order on earth under the personal rule of Jesus Christ, and they would have been amazed if they had learned that this hope was to be motioned out of theology and other ideas substituted.

WE ARE NOT ALONE IN THE FIGHT

For those of us who believe in Jesus Christ, there is [a] . . . sure means of guidance into the future. If the fundamental direction of his mind and his life was a revelation of the will of God for humanity, then he is to us a summons to go forward in the line marked out by him, and also a guarantee that we have the Almighty and his moral universe behind us as we move.

2

The Kingdom of God

THE DOCTRINE OF THE KINGDOM OF GOD

If theology is to offer an adequate doctrinal basis for the social gospel, it must not only make room for the doctrine of the Kingdom of God, but give it a central place and revise all other doctrines so that they will articulate organically with it.

The doctrine is itself the social gospel. Without it, the idea of redeeming the social order will be but an annex to the orthodox conception of the scheme of salvation. It will live like a Negro servant family in a detached cabin back of the white man's house in the South. If this doctrine gets the place which has always been its legitimate right, the practical proclamation and application of social morality will have a firm footing.

To those whose minds live in the social gospel, the Kingdom of God is a dear truth, the marrow of the gospel, just as the incarnation was to Athanasius, justification by faith alone to Luther, and the sovereignty of God to Jonathan Edwards. It was just as dear to Jesus.

He too lived in it, and from it looked out on the world and the work he had to do.

Jesus always spoke of the Kingdom of God. Only two of his reported sayings contain the word "Church," and both passages are of questionable authenticity. It is safe to say that he never thought of founding the kind of institution which afterwards claimed to be acting for him.

Yet immediately after his death, groups of disciples joined and consolidated by inward necessity. Each local group knew that it was part of a divinely founded fellowship mysteriously spreading through humanity, and awaiting the return of the Lord and the establishing of his Kingdom. This universal Church was loved with the same religious faith and reverence with which Jesus had loved the Kingdom of God. It was the partial and earthly realization of the divine Society, and at the Parousia the Church and the Kingdom would merge.

But the Kingdom was merely a hope, the Church a present reality. The chief interest and affection flowed toward the Church. Soon, through a combination of causes, the name and idea of "the Kingdom" began to be displaced by the name and idea of "the Church" in the preaching, literature, and theological thought of the Church. Augustine completed this process in his *De Civitate Dei*. The Kingdom of God which has, throughout human history, opposed the Kingdom of Sin, is today embodied in the Church. The millennium began when the Church was founded. This practically substituted the actual, not the ideal Church for the Kingdom of God. The beloved ideal of Jesus became a vague phrase which kept intruding from the New Testament. Like Cinderella in the kitchen, it saw the other great dogmas furbished up for the ball, but no prince of theology restored it to its rightful place. The Reformation, too, brought no renascence of the doctrine of the Kingdom; it had only eschatological value, or was defined in blurred phrases borrowed from the Church. The present revival of the Kingdom idea is due to the combined influence of the historical study of the Bible and of the social gospel.

When the doctrine of the Kingdom of God shriveled to an undeveloped and pathetic remnant in Christian thought, this loss was bound to have far-reaching consequences. We are told that the loss of a single tooth from the arch of the mouth in childhood may spoil the symmetrical development of the skull and produce malformations affecting the mind and character. The atrophy of that idea which had occupied the chief place in the mind of Jesus necessarily affected the conception of Christianity, the life of the Church, the progress of humanity, and the structure of theology. I shall briefly enumerate some of the consequences affecting theology. This list, however, is by no means complete.

THE CONSEQUENCES OF THE LOSS OF THE KINGDOM OF GOD IDEA

1. Theology lost its contact with the synoptic thought of Jesus. Its problems were not at all the same which

had occupied his mind. It lost his point of view and became to some extent incapable of understanding him. His idea had to be rediscovered in our time. Traditional theology and the mind of Jesus Christ became incommensurable quantities. It claimed to regard his revelation and the substance of his thought as divine, and yet did not learn to think like him. The loss of the Kingdom idea is one key to this situation.

2. The distinctive ethical principles of Jesus were the direct outgrowth of his conception of the Kingdom of God. When the latter disappeared from theology, the former disappeared from ethics. Only persons having the substance of the Kingdom ideal in their minds seem to be able to get relish out of the ethics of Jesus. Only those church bodies which have been in opposition to organized society and have looked for a better city with its foundations in heaven have taken the Sermon on the Mount seriously.

3. The Church is primarily a fellowship for worship; the Kingdom is a fellowship of righteousness. When the latter was neglected in theology, the ethical force of Christianity was weakened; when the former was emphasized in theology, the importance of worship was exaggerated. The prophets and Jesus had cried down sacrifices and ceremonial performances, and cried up righteousness, mercy, solidarity. Theology now reversed this, and by its theoretical discussions did its best to stimulate sacramental actions and priestly importance. Thus the religious energy and enthusiasm which might have saved mankind from its great sins were used up in

hearing and endowing masses, or in maintaining competitive church organizations, while mankind is still stuck in the mud. There are nations in which the ethical condition of the masses is the reverse of the frequency of the masses in the churches.

4. When the Kingdom ceased to be the dominating religious reality, the Church moved up into the position of the supreme good. To promote the power of the Church and its control over all rival political forces was equivalent to promoting the supreme ends of Christianity. This increased the arrogance of churchmen and took the moral check off their policies. For the Kingdom of God can never be promoted by lies, craft, crime, or war, but the wealth and power of the Church have often been promoted by these means. The medieval ideal of the supremacy of the Church over the State was the logical consequence of making the Church the highest good with no superior ethical standard by which to test it. The medieval doctrines concerning the Church and the Papacy were the direct theological outcome of the struggles for Church supremacy, and were meant to be weapons in that struggle.

5. The Kingdom ideal is the test and corrective of the influence of the Church. When the Kingdom ideal disappeared, the conscience of the Church was muffled. It became possible for the missionary expansion of Christianity to halt for centuries without creating any sense of shortcoming. It became possible for the most unjust social conditions to fasten themselves on Christian nations without awakening any consciousness that

the purpose of Christ was being defied and beaten back. The practical undertakings of the Church remained within narrow lines, and the theological thought of the Church was necessarily confined in a similar way. The claims of the Church were allowed to stand in theology with no conditions and obligations to rest and balance them. If the Kingdom had stood as the purpose for which the Church exists, the Church could not have fallen into such corruption and sloth. Theology bears part of the guilt for the pride, the greed, and the ambition of the Church.

6. The Kingdom ideal contains the revolutionary force of Christianity. When this ideal faded out of the systematic thought of the Church, it became a conservative social influence and increased the weight of the other stationary forces in society. If the Kingdom of God had remained part of the theological and Christian consciousness, the Church could not, down to our times, have been salaried by autocratic class governments to keep the democratic and economic impulses of the people under check.

7. Reversely, the movements for democracy and social justice were left without a religious backing for lack of the Kingdom idea. The Kingdom of God as the fellowship of righteousness would be advanced by the abolition of industrial slavery and the disappearance of the slums of civilization; the Church would only indirectly gain through such social changes. Even today many Christians cannot see any religious importance in social justice and fraternity because it does not increase

the number of conversions nor fill the churches. Thus the practical conception of salvation, which is the effective theology of the common man and minister, has been cut back and crippled for lack of the Kingdom ideal.

8. Secular life is belittled as compared with church life. Services rendered to the Church get a higher religious rating than services rendered to the community. Thus the religious value is taken out of the activities of the common man and the prophetic services to society. Wherever the Kingdom of God is a living reality in Christian thought, any advance of social righteousness is seen as a part of redemption and arouses inward joy and the triumphant sense of salvation. When the Church absorbs interest, a subtle asceticism creeps back into our theology and the world looks different.

9. When the doctrine of the Kingdom of God is lacking in theology, the salvation of the individual is seen in its relation to the Church and to the future life, but not in its relation to the task of saving the social order. Theology has left this important point in a condition so hazy and muddled that it has taken us almost a generation to see that the salvation of the individual and the redemption of the social order are closely related, and how.

10. Finally, theology has been deprived of the inspiration of great ideas contained in the idea of the Kingdom and in labor for it. The Kingdom of God breeds prophets; the Church breeds priests and theologians. The Church runs to tradition and dogma; the

Kingdom of God rejoices in forecasts and boundless horizons. The men who have contributed the most fruitful impulses to Christian thought have been men of prophetic vision, and their theology has proved most effective for future times where it has been most concerned with past history, with present social problems, and with the future of human society. The Kingdom of God is to theology what outdoor color and light are to art. It is impossible to estimate what inspirational impulses have been lost to theology and to the Church, because it did not develop the doctrine of the Kingdom of God and see the world and its redemption from that point of view.

These are some of the historical effects which the loss of the doctrine of the Kingdom of God has inflicted on systematic theology. The chief contribution which the social gospel has made and will make to theology is to give new vitality and importance to that doctrine. In doing so it will be a reformatory force of the highest importance in the field of doctrinal theology, for any systematic conception of Christianity must be not only defective but incorrect if the idea of the Kingdom of God does not govern it.

THE DOCTRINE OF THE KINGDOM IS THE THEOLOGY FOR THE SOCIAL GOSPEL

In the following brief propositions I should like to offer a few suggestions, on behalf of the social gospel, for the theological formulation of the doctrine of the

Kingdom. Something like this is needed to give us a theology for the social gospel.

1. The Kingdom of God is divine in its origin, progress, and consummation. It was initiated by Jesus Christ, in whom the prophetic spirit came to its consummation, it is sustained by the Holy Spirit, and it will be brought to its fulfillment by the power of God in his own time. The passive and active resistance of the Kingdom of Evil at every stage of its advance is so great, and the human resources of the Kingdom of God so slender, that no explanation can satisfy a religious mind which does not see the power of God in its movements. The Kingdom of God, therefore, is miraculous all the way, and is the continuous revelation of the power, the righteousness, and the love of God. The establishment of a community of righteousness in mankind is just as much a saving act of God as the salvation of an individual from his natural selfishness and moral inability. The Kingdom of God, therefore, is not merely ethical, but has a rightful place in theology. This doctrine is absolutely necessary to establish that organic union between religion and morality, between theology and ethics, which is one of the characteristics of the Christian religion. When our moral actions are consciously related to the Kingdom of God they gain religious quality. Without this doctrine we shall have expositions of schemes of redemption and we shall have systems of ethics, but we shall not have a true exposition of Christianity. The first step to the reform of the

churches is the restoration of the doctrine of the Kingdom of God.

2. The Kingdom of God contains the teleology of the Christian religion. It translates theology from the static to the dynamic. It sees, not doctrines or rites to be conserved and perpetuated, but resistance to be overcome and great ends to be achieved. Since the Kingdom of God is the supreme purpose of God, we shall understand the Kingdom so far as we understand God, and we shall understand God so far as we understand his Kingdom. As long as organized sin is in the world, the Kingdom of God is characterized by conflict with evil. But if there were no evil, or after evil has been overcome, the Kingdom of God will still be the end to which God is lifting the race. It is realized not only by redemption, but also by the education of mankind and the revelation of his life within it.

3. Since God is in it, the Kingdom of God is always both present and future. Like God it is in all tenses, eternal in the midst of time. It is the energy of God realizing itself in human life. Its future lies among the mysteries of God. It invites and justifies prophecy, but all prophecy is fallible; it is valuable in so far as it grows out of action for the Kingdom and impels action. No theories about the future of the Kingdom of God are likely to be valuable or true which paralyze or postpone redemptive action on our part. To those who postpone, it is a theory and not a reality. It is for us to see the Kingdom of God as always coming, always pressing in on the present, always big with possibility, and always

inviting immediate action. We walk by faith. Every human life is so placed that it can share with God in the creation of the Kingdom, or can resist and retard its progress. The Kingdom is for each of us the supreme task and the supreme gift of God. By accepting it as a task, we experience it as a gift. By laboring for it we enter into the joy and peace of the Kingdom as our divine fatherland and habitation.

4. Even before Christ, men of God saw the Kingdom of God as the great end to which all divine leadings were pointing. Every idealistic interpretation of the world, religious or philosophical, needs some such conception. Within the Christian religion the idea of the Kingdom gets its distinctive interpretation from Christ: (a) Jesus emancipated the idea of the Kingdom from previous nationalistic limitations and from the debasement of lower religious tendencies, and made it world-wide and spiritual. (b) He made the purpose of salvation essential in it. (c) He imposed his own mind, his personality, his love and holy will on the idea of the Kingdom. (d) He not only foretold it but initiated it by his life and work. As humanity more and more develops a racial consciousness in modern life, idealistic interpretations of the destiny of humanity will become more influential and important. Unless theology has a solidaristic vision higher and fuller than any other, it can not maintain the spiritual leadership of mankind, but will be outdistanced. Its business is to infuse the distinctive qualities of Jesus Christ into its teachings

about the Kingdom, and this will be a fresh competitive test of his continued headship of humanity.

5. The Kingdom of God is humanity organized according to the will of God. Interpreting it through the consciousness of Jesus we may affirm these convictions about the ethical relations within the Kingdom: (a) Since Christ revealed the divine worth of life and personality, and since his salvation seeks the restoration and fulfillment of even the least, it follows that the Kingdom of God, at every stage of human development, tends toward a social order which will best guarantee to all personalities their freest and highest development. This involves the redemption of social life from the cramping influence of religious bigotry, from the repression of self-assertion in the relation of upper and lower classes, and from all forms of slavery in which human beings are treated as mere means to serve the ends of others. (b) Since love is the supreme law of Christ, the Kingdom of God implies a progressive reign of love in human affairs. We can see its advance wherever the free will of love supersedes the use of force and legal coercion as a regulative of the social order. This involves the redemption of society from political autocracies and economic oligarchies; the substitution of redemptive for vindictive penology; the abolition of constraint through hunger as part of the industrial system and the abolition of war as the supreme expression of hate and the completest cessation of freedom. (c) The highest expression of love is the free surrender of what is truly our own, life, property, and rights. A much lower but

perhaps more decisive expression of love is the surrender of any opportunity to exploit men. No social group or organization can claim to be clearly within the Kingdom of God which drains others for its own ease, and resists the effort to abate this fundamental evil. This involves the redemption of society from private property in the natural resources of the earth, and from any condition in industry which makes monopoly profits possible. (d) The reign of love tends toward the progressive unity of mankind, but with the maintenance of individual liberty and the opportunity of nations to work out their own national peculiarities and ideals.

DEMOCRATIZING GOD

Here we see one of the highest redemptive services of Jesus to the human race. When he took God by the hand and called him "Our Father," he democratized the conception of God. He disconnected the idea from the coercive and predatory State, and transferred it to the realm of family life, the chief social embodiment of solidarity and love. He not only saved humanity; he saved God. He gave God his first chance of being loved and of escaping from the worst misunderstandings conceivable. The value of Christ's idea of the Fatherhood of God is realized only by contrast to the despotic ideas which it opposed and was meant to displace. We have classified theology as Greek and Latin, as Catholic and Protestant. It is time to classify it as despotic and democratic. From a Christian point of view that is a more decisive distinction.

God is the common basis of all our life. Our human personalities may seem distinct, but their roots run down into the eternal life of God. In a large way both philosophy and science are tending toward a recognition of the truth which religion has felt and practiced. The all-pervading life of God is the ground of the spiritual oneness of the race and of our hope for its closer fellowship in the future.

The consciousness of solidarity, therefore, is of the essence of religion. But the circumference and spaciousness of the fellowship within it differ widely. Every discovery of a larger fellowship by the individual brings a glow of religious satisfaction. The origin of the Christian religion was bound up with a great transition from a nationalistic to an international religious consciousness. Paul was the hero of that conquest. The Christian God has been a breaker of barriers from the first. All who have a distinctively Christian experience of God are committed to the expansion of human fellowships and to the overthrow of barriers. To emphasize this and bring it home to the Christian consciousness is part of the mission of the social gospel, and it looks to theology for the intellectual formulation of what it needs.

DEMOCRATIZING THE HOLY SPIRIT

But in fact the social nature of religion is clearly demonstrated in the work of the Holy Spirit. The prophets of the Old Testament were not lonely torches set aflame by the spirit of God; they were more like a string of electric lights along a roadside which, though

far apart, are all connected and caused by the same current. They transmitted not only their ideas but their spiritual receptivity and inspiration to one another.

The Christian Church began its history as a community of inspiration. The new thing in the story of Pentecost is not only the number of those who received the tongue of fire but the fact that the Holy Spirit had become the common property of a group. What had seemed to some extent the privilege of aristocratic souls was now democratized. The spirit was poured on all flesh; the young saw visions, the old dreamed dreams; even on the slave class the spirit was poured. The charismatic life of the primitive Church was highly important for its coherence and loyalty in the crucial days of its beginning. It was a chief feeder of its strong affections, its power of testimony, and its sacrificial spirit. Religion has been defined as "the life of God in the soul of men." In Christianity it became also the life of God in the fellowship of man. The mystic experience was socialized.

THE KINGDOM OF GOD AS LOVE AND LABOR

Two aspects of the Kingdom of God demand special considerations in this connection: the Kingdom is the realm of love, and it is the commonwealth of labor.

Jesus Christ superimposed his own personality on the previous conception of God and made love the distinctive characteristic of God and the supreme law of human conduct. Consequently the reign of God would be the reign of love. It is not enough to think of the Kingdom as a prevalence of good will. The institutions of life must be fundamentally fraternal and co-operative if they are to train men to love their fellow-men as co-workers. Sin, being selfish, is covetous and grasping. It favors institutions and laws which permit unrestricted exploitation and accumulation. This in turn sets up antagonistic interests, increases lawsuits, class hostility, and wars, and so miseducates mankind that love and co-operation seem unworkable, and men are taught to put their trust in coercive control by the strong and in the sting of hunger and compulsion for the poor.

Being the realm of love, the Kingdom of God must also be the commonwealth of co-operative labor, for how can we actively love others without serving their needs by our abilities? If the Kingdom of God is a community of highly developed personalities, it must also be an organization for labor, for none can realize himself fully without labor. A divinely ordered community, therefore, would offer to all the opportunities of education and employment, and expect from all their contribution of labor.

THE KINGDOM COMES BY SLOW GROWTH

The popular conception expected the new age to come by divine miraculous interference simply. The Messiah would descend from heaven with angelic legions, expel the Romans, judge the nation, punish the apostate Jews, and then the new Jerusalem, which was already complete and waiting in heaven, would descend from above. That was the Utopia of Jewish apocalypticism. Jesus never eliminated the direct acts of God and the significance of divine catastrophes from his outlook. But in his parables taken from biological processes he developed a conception of continuous and quiet growth, culminating at last in the judgment act of God. The Kingdom of God, he said, is like a farmer who sows his grain and lets the forces of nature work; he goes about his daily tasks, and all the time the tiny blades come up, the ear forms and gets heavy, and then comes the harvest.

Jesus was working his way toward evolutionary conceptions. They were so new to his followers that he put them in parable form to avoid antagonism.

Such a conception of the Kingdom brought it closer to human action. It was already at work; it was in one sense already present. It was possible then to help it along.

3

The Social Principles of Jesus

ALL ARE CHILDREN OF GOD

Love and religion have the power of idealistic interpretation. To a mother her child is a wonderful being. To a true lover the girl he loves has sacredness. With Jesus the consciousness of a God of love revealed the beauty of men. The old gods were despotic supermen, mythical duplicates of the human kings and conquerors. The God of Jesus was the great Father who lets his light shine on the just and the unjust, and offers forgiveness and love to all. Jesus lived in the spiritual atmosphere of that faith. Consequently he saw men from that point of view. They were to him children of that God. Even the lowliest was high. The light that shone on him from the face of God shed a splendor on the prosaic ranks of men. In this way religion enriches and illuminates social feeling.

"Jesus Christ was the first to bring the value of every human soul to light, and what he did no one can any more undo" (Harnack). But it remains for every individual to accept and reaffirm that religious faith as his own guiding principle according to which he proposes to live. We shall be at one with the spirit of Christianity and of modern civilization if we approach all men with the expectation of finding beneath commonplace, sordid, or even repulsive externals some qualities of love, loyalty, heroism, aspiration, or repentance, which prove the divine in man. Kant expressed that reverence for personality in his doctrine that we must never treat a man as a means only, but always as an end in himself. So far as our civilization treats men merely as labor force, fit to produce wealth for the few, it is not yet Christian. Any man who treats his fellows in that way blunts his higher nature; as Fichte says, whoever treats another as a slave, becomes a slave. We might add, whoever treats him as a child of God, becomes a child of God and learns to know God.

Jesus saw a moral solidarity existing, not only between contemporaries who act together, but between generations that act alike. Every generation clings to its profitable wrongs and tries to silence those who stand for higher righteousness. Posterity takes comfort in being fairer about the dead issues, but is just as hot and bad about present issues. The sons re-enact the old tragedies on a new stage, and so line up with their fathers. In looking back over the history of his nation, Jesus saw a continuity of wrong which bound the generations together in a solidarity of guilt.

That man is a social being is the fundamental fact with which all social sciences have to deal. We may like or dislike people; we can not well be indifferent to them if they get close to us. As Sartor Resartus puts it: "In vain thou deniest it; thou *art* my brother. Thy very hatred, thy very envy, those foolish lies thou tellest of me in thy splenetic humour; what is all this but an inverted sympathy? Were I a steam-engine, wouldst thou take the trouble to tell lies of me?"

Sex admiration, parental love, the dear love of comrades, the thrill of patriotism, the joy of play, are all forms of fellowship. They give us happiness because they satisfy our social instinct. To realize our unity gives relish to life. To be thrust out of fellowship is the great pain. Many evil things get their attractiveness mainly through the fact that they create a bit of fellowship—such as it is. The slender thread of good in the saloon is comradeship.

None ever felt this social unity of our race more deeply than Jesus. To him it was sacred and divine. Hence his emphasis on love and forgiveness. He put his personality behind the natural instinct of social attraction and encouraged it. He swung the great force of religion around to bear on it and drive it home. Anything that substitutes antagonism for fraternity is evil to him. Just as in the case of the natural respect for human life and personality, so in the case of the natural social cohesion of men, he lifted the blind instinct of human nature by the insight of religion and constituted it a fundamental principle of life. It is the business of Christianity to widen the area of comradeship.

Common human judgment assents to the valuation of Jesus. Wherever an effective and stable form of fellowship has been created, a sense of sacredness begins to attach to it, and men defend it as a sort of shrine of the divine in man. Wherever men are striving to create a larger fellowship, they have religious enthusiasm as if they were building a temple for God. This is the heart of church loyalty.

EACH PERSON IS VALUABLE

Whenever Jesus looked at any man singly, he saw and felt his divine worth, not on account of anything the man owned and knew, but on account of his humanity. The child, the cripple, the harlot, were to him something precious and holy, and he stood at bay over them when anyone tried to trample on them in the name of property, respectability, or religion. He was always moving to break down the power of sin in the individual and of wrong in society, which corrupted or crushed this divine worth, and to furnish a faith, a spirit, a motive, and a human environment in which the life of man could unfold in freedom and strength.

WE BELONG TOGETHER

Whenever Jesus looked at men collectively, he saw and felt their unity and brotherhood. To him sin consists in that which divides, in war and hate, in pride and lies, in injustice and greed. Salvation consists in drawing together in love, as children of one Father. If any member of the human family is weak or perishing, it concerns all. The solidarity of mankind was the great conviction underneath all his teachings.

SOLIDARITY OF FAMILY AND NATION

The family is the most striking case of solidarity. It is first formed of two units at opposite poles in point of sex, experience, taste, need, and aims; and when they form it, they usually have as much sense of sacredness as their character is capable of feeling. When children are added, more divergences of age, capacity, and need are injected. Yet out of these contradictory elements a social fellowship is built up, which, in the majority of cases, defies the shocks of life and the strain of changing moods and needs, forms the chief source of contentment for the majority of men and women, and, when conspicuously successful, wins the spontaneous tribute of reverence from all right-thinking persons.

Political unity was at first an expansion of family unity. The passionate loyalty with which a nation defends its country and its freedom is not simply a defense of real estate and livestock, but of its national brotherhood and solidarity. The devotion with which people suffer and die for their State is all the more remarkable because all States hitherto have been largely organizations for coercion and exploitation, and only in part real fraternal communities. Patriotism hitherto has been largely a prophetic outreaching toward a great fellowship nowhere realized. The peoples walk by faith.

EQUALITY THE FOUNDATION OF POLITICAL DEMOCRACY

Approximate equality is the only enduring foundation of political democracy. The sense of equality is the only basis for Christian morality. Healthful human relations seem to run only on horizontal lines. Consequently true love always seeks to create a level. If a rich man loves a poor girl, he lifts her to financial and social equality with himself. If his love has not that equalizing power, it is flawed and becomes prostitution. Wherever husbands by social custom regard their wives as inferior, there is a deep-seated defect in married life. If a teacher talks down at his pupils, not as a maturer friend, but with an "I say so," he confines their minds in a spiritual strait jacket instead of liberating them. Equality is the only basis for true educational influences. Even our instinct of pity, which is love going out to the weak, works with spontaneous strength only toward those of our own class and circle who have dropped into misfortune. Businessmen feel very differently toward the widow of a businessman left in poverty than they do toward a widow of the poorer classes. People of the lower class who demand our help are "cases"; people of our own class are folks.

The demand for equality is often ridiculed as if it implied that all men were to be of identical wealth, wisdom, and authority. But social equality can coexist with the greatest natural differences. There is no more fundamental difference than that of sex, nor a greater intellectual chasm than that between an educ[illegible] and his little child, yet in the family all are eq[illegible] a college community there are various gradations of rank and authority within the faculty, and there is a clearly marked distinction between the students and the faculty, but there is social equality. On the other hand, the janitor and the peanut vender are outside of the circle, however important they may be to it.

The social equality existing in our country in the past has been one of the chief charms of life here and of far more practical importance to our democracy than the universal ballot. After a long period of study abroad in my youth I realized on my return to America that life here was far poorer in music, art, and many forms of enjoyment than life on the continent of Europe; but that life tasted better here, nevertheless, because men met one another more simply, frankly, and wholesomely. In Europe a man is always considering just how much deference he must show to those in ranks above him, and in turn noting jealously if those below him are strewing the right quantity of incense due to his own social position.

Christianity gave a new valuation to the quality of humility in ethics. Humility is the sense of dependence on others, the feeling that whatever we have has been received from God and our fellow-men, and that we find our true life only as serviceable members of the social organism. But wealth emancipates from that sense of dependence. Unless religion counteracts it, it displaces humility by pride. But therewith the rich be-

come unavailable for social service, and a danger to the society that has equipped them with their wealth.

THE CONSCIOUSNESS OF HUMANITY MUST BE ACHIEVED

It is one thing to praise love and another thing to practice it. We may theorize about society, and ourselves be contrary and selfish units in it. Society unity is an achievement. A loving mind toward our fellows, even the cranky, is the prize of a lifetime. How can it be evoked and cultivated in us? That is one of the most important problems in education. Can it be solved without religious influences? Love will not up at the bidding. We can observe the fact that pearsonal dicipleship of Christ has given some persons in our acquaintance a rare capacity for love, for social sympathy, for peaceableness, for all the society-making qualities. We can make test of the fact for ourselves that every real contact with him gives us an accession of fraternity and greater fitness for noble social unity. It makes us good fellows.

The man who intelligently realizes the Chinese and the Zulu as his brothers with whom he must share the earth is an ampler mind—other things being equal—than the man who can think of humanity only in terms of pale-faces. The consciousness of humanity will have to be wrought out just as the consciousness of nationality was gradually acquired. He who has it is ahead of his time and a pioneer of the future. The missionary puts himself in the position to acquire that wider sense of solidarity. By becoming a neighbor to remote people he broadens their conception of humanity and his own, and then can be an interpreter of his new friends to his old friends. The interest in foreign missions has, in fact, been a prime educational force, carrying a world-wide consciousness of solidarity into thousands of plain minds and homes that would otherwise have been provincial in their horizon.

A world-wide civilization must have a common monotheistic faith as its spiritual basis. Such a faith must be unitive and not divisive. What the world needs is a religion with a powerful sense of solidarity.

Was Jesus the Coming One? He did not quite measure up to John's expectations. The Messiah was to purge the people of evil elements, winnowing the chaff from the wheat and burning it. His symbol was the axe. Jesus was manifesting no such spirit. Was he then the Messiah?

Jesus shifted the test to another field. Human suffering was being relieved and the poor were having glad news proclaimed to them. Sympathy for the people was the assured common ground between Jesus and John. Jesus felt that John would recognize the dawn of the reign of God by the evidence which he offered him.

No one can turn from a frank reading of the gospels without realizing that Jesus had a deep fellow-feeling, not only for suffering and handicapped individuals, but for the mass of the poorer people of his country, the peasants, the fishermen, the artisans. He declared that it was his mission to bring glad tidings to this class;

and not only glad words, but happy realities. Evidently the expectation of the coming reign of God to his mind signified some substantial relief and release to the submerged and oppressed. Our modern human feeling glories in this side of our Saviour's work. Art and literature love to see him from this angle.

His concern for the poor was the necessary result of the two fundamental convictions discussed by us in the previous chapters. If he felt the sacredness of life even in its humble and hardworn forms, and if he felt the family unity of all men in such a way that the sorrows of the poor were his sorrows, then, of course, he could not be at ease while the people were skinned and prostrate, like sheep without a shepherd. Wherever any group has developed real solidarity, its best attention is always given to those who are most in need. "The whole have no need of a physician," said Jesus; the strong can take care of themselves.

So he cast in his lot with the people consciously. He slept in their homes, healed their diseases, ate their bread, and shared his own with them. He gave them a faith, a hope of better days, and a sense that God was on their side. Such a faith is more than meat and drink. In turn they rallied around him, and could not get enough of him. The common people heard him gladly.

JESUS TRUSTED AND LOVED THE "COMMON PEOPLE"

Furthermore, the feeling of Jesus for the poor was not the sort of compassion we feel for the hopelessly crippled in body or mind. His feeling was one of love and trust. The Galilean peasants, from whom Peter and John sprang, were not morons, or the sodden dregs of city slums. They were the patient, hard-working folks who have always made up the rank and file of all peoples. They had their faults, and Jesus must have known them. But did he ever denounce them, or call them offspring of vipers? Did he ever indicate that their special vices were frustrating the Kingdom of God? They needed spiritual impulse and leadership, but their nature was sound and they were the raw material for the redeemed humanity which he strove to create.

There is one more quality which we shall have to recognize in the attitude of Jesus to the poor. He saw them over against the rich. Amid all the variations of human society these two groups always reappear—those who live by their own productive labor, and those who live on the productive labor of others whom they control. Practically they overlap and blend, but when our perspective is distant enough, we can distinguish them. In Greek and Roman society, in medieval life, and in all civilized nations of today—barring, of course, our own—we can see them side by side. Each conditions the other; neither would exist without the other. Each class develops its own moral and spiritual habits, its own set of virtues and vices. Some of us were born in the upper class, some in the lower; and in college groups the majority come from the border line. By instinct, by the experiences of life, or by national reflection, we usually give our moral allegiance to one or the other, and are then apt to lean to that side in every question arising.

Now Jesus took sides with the group of toil. He stood up for them. He stood with them. We can not help seeing him with his arm thrown in protection about the poor man, and his other hand raised in warning to the rich. If we are in any doubt about this, we can let his contemporaries decide it for us. Plainly the common people claimed him as their friend. Did the governing classes have the same feeling for him? It seems hard to escape the conclusion that Jesus was not impartial between the two. Was he nevertheless just? To the aesthetic sense, and also to the superficial moral judgment, the upper classes are everywhere more congenial and attractive. To the moral judgment of Jesus . . . there was something disquieting and dangerous about the spiritual qualities of the rich, and something lovable and hopeful about the qualities of the common man. Was he right? This is a very important practical question for all who are disposed to follow his moral leadership.

THE HEBREW PROPHETS AND THE "COMMON PEOPLE"

We shall get the historical setting for Christ's championship of the people by going back to the Old Testament prophets. They were his spiritual forebears. He nourished his mind on their writings and loved to quote them. Now the Hebrew prophets with one accord stood up for the common people and laid the blame for social wrong on the powerful classes. They underlined no other sin with such scarlet marks as the sins of injustice, oppression, and the corruption of judges. But these are the sins which bear down the lowly, and have always been practiced and hushed up by the powerful.

> Hear this word, ye kine of Bashan, that oppress the poor, that crush the needy. . . . Ye trample upon the poor, and take exactions from him of wheat; . . . ye that afflict the just, that take a bribe, and that turn aside the needy in the gate from their right. . . . For three transgressions of Israel, yea, for four, I will not turn away the punishment thereof; because they have sold the righteous for silver, and the needy for a pair of shoes; they that pant after the dust of the earth on the head of the poor.—Amos 4:1; 5:11-12; 2:6-7.

Micah describes the strong and crafty crowding the peasant from his ancestral holding and the mother from her home by the devices always used for such ends: exorbitant interest on loans, foreclosure in times of distress, "seeing the judge" before the trial, and hardness of heart toward broken life and happiness. We can not belittle the moral insight of that unique succession of men. Their spiritual force is still hard at work in our Christian civilization, especially in the contribution which the Jewish people are making to the labor movement.

THERE ARE NONE BENEATH HIS CARE

And they were bringing unto him little children, that he should touch them: and the disciples rebuked them.

But when Jesus saw it, he was moved with indignation, and said unto them, Suffer the little children to come unto me; forbid them not: for to such belongeth the Kingdom of God. Verily I say unto you, Whosoever shall not receive the Kingdom of God as a little child, he shall in no wise enter therein. And he took them in his arms, and blessed them, laying his hands upon them. —Mark 10:13-16.

The child is humanity reduced to its simplest terms. Affectionate joy in children is perhaps the purest expression of social feeling. Jesus was indignant when the disciples thought children were not of sufficient importance to occupy his attention. Compared with the selfish ambition of grownups he felt something heavenly in children, a breath of the Kingdom of God. They are nearer the Kingdom than those whom the world has smudged. To inflict any spiritual injury on one of these little ones seemed to him an inexpressible guilt.

JESUS RECOGNIZES NO SOCIAL BARRIERS

Now all the publicans and sinners were drawing near unto him to hear him. And both the Pharisees and the scribes murmured, saying, This man receiveth sinners, and eateth with them.

And he spake unto them this parable, saying, What man of you, having a hundred sheep, and having lost one of them, doth not leave that ninety and nine in the wilderness, and go after that which is lost, until he find it? And when he hath found it, he layeth it on his shoulders, rejoicing. And when he cometh home, he calleth together his friends and his neighbors, saying unto them, Rejoice with me, for I have found my sheep which was lost. I say unto you, that even so there shall be joy in heaven over one sinner that repenteth, more than over ninety and nine righteous persons, who need no repentance.

Or what woman having ten pieces of silver, if she lose one piece, doth not light a lamp, and sweep the house, and seek diligently until she find it? And when she hath found it, she calleth together her friends and neighbors, saying, Rejoice with me, for I have found the piece which I had lost. Even so, I say unto you, there is joy in the presence of the angels of God over one sinner that repenteth.—Luke 15:1-10.

Every Jewish community had a fringe of unchurched people, who could not keep up the strict observance of the law and had given up trying. The pious people, just because they were pious, felt they must cold-shoulder such. Jesus walked across the lines established.

Here Jesus formulates the inner meaning and mission of his life as he himself felt it. He was here for social restoration and moral salvage. No human being should go to pieces if he could help it. He was not only willing to help people who came to him for help, but he proposed to go after them. The "lost" man was too valuable and sacred to be lost.

DOING MORE THAN JUSTICE REQUIRES

For the kingdom of heaven is like unto a man that was a householder, who went out early in the morning to hire laborers into his vineyard. And when he had agreed with the laborers for a shilling a day, he sent them into his vineyard. And he went out about the third hour, and saw others standing in the market place idle; and to them he said, Go ye also into the vineyard, and whatsoever is right I will give you. And they went their way. Again he went out about the sixth and the ninth hour, and did likewise. And about the eleventh hour he went out and found others standing: and he saith unto them, Why stand ye here all the day idle? They say unto him, Because no man hath hired us. He said unto them, Go ye also into the vineyard. And when even was come, the lord of the vineyard said unto his steward, Call the laborers, and pay them their hire, beginning from the last unto the first. And when they came that were hired about the eleventh hour, they received every man a shilling. And when the first came, they supposed that they would receive more; and they likewise received every man a shilling. And when they received it, they murmured against the householder, saying, These last have spent but one hour, and thou hast made them equal unto us, who have borne the burden of the day and the scorching heat. But he answered and said to one of them, Friend, I do thee no wrong: didst not thou agree with me for a shilling? Take up that which is thine, and go thy way; it is my will to give unto this last, even as unto thee. Is it not lawful for me to do what I will with mine own? or is thine eye evil, because I am good? So the last shall be first, and the first last.—Matt. 20:1-16.

Judaism rested on legality. So much obedience to the law earned so much reward, according to the contract between God and Israel. Theoretically this was just; practically it gave the inside track to the respectable and well-to-do, for it took leisure and money to obey the minutiae of the law. In this parable the employer rises from the level of justice to the higher plane of human fellow-feeling. These eleventh-hour men had been ready to work; they had to eat and live; he proposed to give them a living wage because he felt an inner prompting to do so. In the parable of the Prodigal Son the father does more for his son than justice required, because he was a father. Here the employer does more because he is a man. Each acted from a sense of the worth of the human life with which he was dealing. It was the same sense of worth and sacredness in Jesus which prompted him to invent these parables.

SOCIAL EVOLUTION MOVES TOWARD JESUS

In recent centuries the vast forces of social evolution seem to have set in the direction toward which Jesus faced. Since the Reformation the institutions of religion have more or less democratized. The common people have secured some participation in political power and have been able to use it somewhat for their economic betterment. They share much more fully in education than formerly. Before the outbreak of the Great War it seemed safe to anticipate that the working people would secure an increasing share of social wealth, the security, the opportunities for health, for artistic enjoyment, and of all that makes life worth living. Today the future is heavily clouded and uncertain; but our faith still holds that even the great disaster will help ultimately to weaken the despotic and exploiting forces, and make the condition of the common people more than ever the chief concern of science and statesmanship.

Jesus was on the side of the common people long before democracy was on the ascendant. He loved them, felt their worth, trusted their latent capacities, and promised them the Kingdom of God. The religion he founded, even when impure and under the control of the upper classes, has been the historical basis for the aspirations of the common people and has readily united with democratic movements. His personality and spirit has remained an impelling and directing force in the minds of many individuals who have "gone to the people" because they know Jesus is with them. In fact we can look for more direct social effectiveness of Jesus in the future, because the new historical interpretation of the Bible helps us to see him more plainly amid the social life of his own people.

FACE THE FACTS AND REPENT

The ABC of social renewal and moral advance is for each of us to face our sin sincerely and get on a basis of frankness with God and ourselves. Therefore Christianity set out with a call for personal repentance. If we only acted up to what we know to be right, this world would be a different place. But we fool ourselves with protective coloring devices in order to keep our own self-respect. Take our language, for instance; it reeks with evasive euphemisms intended to make nasty sins look prettier. We call stealing "swiping" and cheating "cribbing." . . . As soon as we face the facts, we realize that what we call peccadilloes in ourselves are the black sins that have slain the innocents and have hagridden humanity through all its history. That is the beginning of social vision. Personal repentance is a social advance.

JESUS COMBINES CONSERVATISM AND RADICALISM

The most obvious duty was for every man to clean up his own backyard and repent of his sins. Everyone should approximate the life of the Kingdom by living now as he would expect to live then. But, as we have seen from his sayings, Jesus went far beyond this. He demanded an elevation of the accepted ethical standards. It was not simply a matter of erring and lagging individuals, but of the socialized norms of conduct. He had deep reverence and loyalty for the religion of his nation, and never told his followers to break with it. But he asserted boldly that the customary ethics of Judaism, based on the Decalogue and its interpretation by the Jewish theologians, was not good enough. It was good as far as it went, and he had no destructive criticism of it, but it needed to be "fulfilled" and to have its lines prolonged.

THE SOCIAL PRINCIPLES IN LEADERSHIP

Then came to him the mother of the sons of Zebedee with her sons, worshipping him, and asking a certain thing of him. And he said unto her, What wouldest thou? She said unto him, Command that these my two sons may sit, one on thy right hand, and one on th left hand, in thy kingdom. But Jesus answered and saic Ye know not what ye ask. Are ye able to drink the cu that I am about to drink? They say unto him, We are able. He saith unto them, My cup indeed ye shall drink: but to sit on my right hand, and on my left hand, is not mine to give; but it is for them for whom it hath been prepared of my Father. And when the ten heard it, they were moved with indignation concerning the two brethren. But Jesus called them unto him, and said, Ye know that the rulers of the Gentiles lord it over them, and their great ones exercise authority over them. Not so shall it be among you: but whosoever would become great among you shall be your minister; and whosoever would be first among you shall be your servant: even as the Son of man came not to be ministered unto, but to minister, and to give his life a ransom for many.—Matt. 20:20-28.

This passage is fundamental for our subject. It is the clearest formulation of the social principle involved in leadership. It contrasts two opposite types of leadership throughout human history. Salome and her sons thought Jesus was going to Jerusalem to inaugurate his Kingdom. They asked for an advance pledge assuring them of the chief place. Jesus replied that that place would not go by favoritism. There is a price to be paid for leadership in his reign, and God alone will allot the final honors. He felt in their request a relapse into conceptions that he detested. In all political organizations he saw the tyrannical use of power over the people. There must be an end of that in the new social order. Ambition must seek its satisfaction by distinguished service, and only extra-hazardous service shall win honor. He himself proposed to be a leader of that new type, and to give his life as a ransom for the emancipation of the people.

THE REDEMPTION OF THE ACQUISITIVE INSTINCT

And one out of the multitude said unto him, Teacher, bid my brother divide the inheritance with me. But he said unto him, Man, who made me a judge or a divider over you? And he said unto them, Take heed, and keep yourselves from all covetousness: for a man's life consisteth not in the abundance of the things which he possesseth. And he spake a parable unto them, saying, The ground of a certain rich man brought forth plentifully: and he reasoned within himself, saying, What shall I do, because I have not where to bestow my fruits? And he said, This will I do: I will pull down my barns, and build greater; and there will I bestow all my grain and my goods. And I will say to my soul, Soul, thou hast much goods laid up for many years; take thine ease, eat, drink, be merry. But God said unto him, Thou foolish one, this night is thy soul required of thee; and the things which thou hast prepared, whose shall they be? So is he that layeth up treasure for himself, and is not rich toward God.—Luke 12:13-21.

Most men today would have no fault to find with this man. He was only doing what the modern world is unanimously trying to do. Having made a pile, he proposed to make a bigger pile. Meanwhile he slapped his soul on the back and smacked his lips in anticipation. To Jesus the fat farmer was a tragic comedy. In the first place, an unseen hand was waiting to snuff out his candle. To plan life as if it consisted in an abundance of material wealth is something of a miscalculation in a world where death is part of the scheme of things. In the second place, Jesus saw no higher purpose in the man's aim and outlook to redeem his acquisitiveness. The man was a sublimated chipmunk, gloating over bushels of pignuts. If wealth is saved to raise and educate children, or achieve some social good, it deserves moral respect or admiration. But if the acquisitive instinct is without social feeling or vision, and centered on self, it gets no respect, at least from Jesus.

INDIFFERENCE TO HUMAN NEED IS SIN

Now there was a certain rich man, and he was clothed in purple and fine linen, faring sumptuously every day: and a certain beggar named Lazarus was laid at his gate, full of sores, and desiring to be fed with the crumbs that fell from the rich man's table; yea, even the dogs came and licked his sores. And it came to pass, that the beggar died, and that he was carried away by the angels into Abraham's bosom: and the rich man also died, and was buried. And in Hades he lifted up his eyes, being in torments, and seeth Abraham afar off, and Lazarus in his bosom. And he cried and said, Father Abraham, have mercy on me, and send Lazarus, that he may dip the tip of his finger in water, and cool my tongue; for I am in anguish in this flame. But Abraham said, Son, remember that thou in thy lifetime receivedst thy good things, and Lazarus in like manner evil things: but now here he is comforted, and thou art in anguish. And besides all this, between us and you there is a great gulf fixed, that they would pass from hence to you may not be able, and that none may cross over from thence to us. And he said, I pray thee therefore, Father, that thou wouldest send him to my father's house; for I have five brethren; that he may testify unto them, lest they also come into this place of torment. But Abraham saith, They have Moses and the prophets; let them hear them. And he said, Nay, Father Abraham: but if one go to them from the dead, they will repent. And he said unto him, If they hear not Moses and the prophets, neither will they be persuaded, if one rise from the dead.—Luke 16:19-21.

Why does Jesus send the rich man to hell as if it were a matter of course? No crimes or vices are alleged. It must be that a life given over to sumptuous living and indifferent to the want and misery of a fellow-man at the doorstep seemed to Jesus a deeply immoral and sinful life. Jesus exerted all his energies to bring men close together in love. But wealth divides. It creates semihuman relations between social classes, so that a small dole seems to be a full discharge of obligations toward the poor, and manly independence and virtue may be resented as offensive. The sting of this parable is in the reference to the five brothers who were still living as Dives had lived, and whom he was vainly trying to reach by wireless.

WE ARE WHAT WE DO

Either make the tree good, and its fruit good; or make the tree corrupt, and its fruit corrupt: for the tree is known by its fruit. Ye offspring of vipers, how can ye, being evil, speak good things? for out of the abundance of the heart the mouth speaketh. The good man out of his good treasure bringeth forth good things: and the evil man out of his evil treasure bringeth forth evil things. And I say unto you, that every idle word that men shall speak, they shall give account thereof in the day of judgment. For by thy words thou shalt be justified, and by thy words thou shalt be condemned.—Matt. 12:33-37.

Character is formed by action, but after it is formed, it determines action. What a man says and does, he becomes; and what he has become, he says and does. An honest and clean-minded man instinctively does what is kind and honorable. But when a man for years has gone for profit and selfish power, you can trust him as a general thing to do what is underhanded and mean. Since selfish ability elbows its way to controlling positions in business, politics, and society, the character reactions of such men are a force with which the Kingdom of God must reckon. They are the personal equipment of the kingdom of evil, and the more respectable, well-dressed, and clever they are, the worse it is.

4

Sin: Its Reality and Power

THE NATURE OF SIN

It is not easy to define sin, for sin is as elastic and complicated as life itself. Its quality, degree, and culpability vary according to the moral intelligence and maturity of the individual, according to his social freedom, and his power over others. Theologians have erred, it seems to me, by fitting the definitions to the most highly developed forms of sin and then spreading them over germinal and semisinful actions and conditions.

We are equipped with powerful appetites. We are often placed in difficult situations, which constitute overwhelming temptations. We are all relatively ignorant, and while we experiment with life, we go astray. Some of our instincts may become rampant and overgrown, and then trample on our inward freedom. We are gifted with high ideals, with a wonderful range of possibilities, with aspiration and longing, and also weighted with inertia and moral incapacity to achieve. We are keenly alive to the call of the senses and the pleasures of the moment, and only dimly and occasionally conscious of our own higher destiny, of the mystic value of personality in others, and of God.

This sensual equipment, this ignorance and inertia, out of which our moral delinquencies sprout, are part of our human nature. We did not order it so. Instead of increasing our guilt, our make-up seems to entitle us to the forbearing judgment of every onlooker, especially God. Yet no doubt we are involved in objective wrong and evil; we frustrate our possibilities; we injure others, we disturb the divine harmonies. We are unfree, unhappy, conscious of a burden which we are unable to lift or escape.

Sin becomes guilt in the full sense in the degree in which intelligence and will enter. We have the impulse to live our life, to exercise our freedom, to express and satisfy the limitless cravings in us, and we are impatient of restraint. We know that our idleness or sensuality will cripple our higher self, yet we want what we want. We set our desires against the rights of others, and disregard the claims of mercy, of gratitude, or of parental love. Our self-love is wrought up to hot ill-will, hate, lying, slander, and malevolence. Men press their covetousness to the injury of society. They are willing to frustrate the cause of liberty and social justice in whole nations in order to hold their selfish social and economic privileges. Men who were powerful enough to do so have left broad trails of destruction and enslavement through history in order to satisfy their selfish caprice, avarice, and thirst for glory.

Two things strike us as we thus consider the development of sin from its cotyledon leaves to its blossom and fruit. First, that the element of selfishness emerges as the character of sin matures. Second, that in the higher forms of sin it assumes the aspect of a conflict between the selfish ego and the common good of humanity; or, expressing it in religious terms, it becomes a conflict between self and God.

The three forms of sin—sensuousness, selfishness, and godlessness—are ascending and expanding stages, in which we sin against our higher self, against the good of men, and against the universal good.

Theology with remarkable unanimity has discerned that sin is essentially selfishness. This is an ethical and social definition, and is proof of the unquenchable social spirit of Christianity. It is more essentially Christian than the dualistic conception of the Greek Fathers, who thought of sin as fundamentally sensuousness and materiality, and saw the chief consequence of the fall in the present reign of death rather than in the reign of selfishness.

The definition of sin as selfishness furnishes an excellent theological basis for a social conception of sin and salvation. But the social gospel can contribute a good deal to socialize and vitalize it.

Theology pictures the self-affirmation of the sinner as a sort of solitary duel of the will between him and God. We get a mental image of God sitting on his throne in glory, holy and benevolent, and the sinner down below, sullenly shaking his fist at God while he repudiates the divine will and chooses his own. Now, in actual life such titanic rebellion against the Almighty is rare. Perhaps our Puritan forefathers knew more cases than we because their theological God was accustomed to issue arbitrary decrees which invited rebellion. We do not rebel; we dodge and evade. We kneel in lowly submission and kick our duty under the bed while God is not looking.

SIN IS AGAINST GOD AND HUMANITY

The theological definitions of sin have too much the flavor of the monarchical institutions under the spiritual influence of which they were first formed. In an absolute monarchy the first duty is to bow to the royal will. A man may spear peasants or outrage their wives, but crossing the king is another matter. When theological definitions speak of rebellion against God as the common characteristic of all sin, it reminds one of the readiness of despotic governments to treat every offense as treason.

Sin is not a private transaction between the sinner and God. Humanity always crowds the audience room when God holds court. We must democratize the conception of God; then the definition of sin will become more realistic.

We love and serve God when we love and serve our fellows, whom he loves and in whom he lives. We rebel against God and repudiate his will when we set our profit and ambition above the welfare of our fellows and above the Kingdom of God which binds them together.

We rarely sin against God alone. The Decalogue gives a simple illustration of this. Theology used to distinguish between the first and second table of the Decalogue; the first enumerated the sins against God and the second the sins against men. Jesus took the Sabbath commandment off the first table and added it to the second; he said the Sabbath is not a taboo day of God, but an institution for the good of man. The command to honor our parents is also ethical. There remain the first three commandments, against polytheism, image worship, and the misuse of the holy name. The worship of various gods and the use of idols is no longer one of our dangers. The misuse of the holy name has lost much of its religious significance since sorcery and magic have moved to the back streets. On the other hand, the commandments of the second table grow more important all the time. Science supplies the means of killing, finance the methods of stealing, the newspapers have learned how to bear false witness artistically to a globeful of people daily, and covetousness is the moral basis of our civilization.

GOD AND HUMANITY ARE INSEPARABLE

God is not only the spiritual representative of humanity; he is identified with it. In him we live and move and have our being. In us he lives and moves, though his being transcends ours. He is the life and light in every man and the mystic bond that unites us all. He is the spiritual power behind and beneath all our aspirations and achievements. He works through humanity to realize his purposes, and our sins block and destroy the reign of God in which he might fully reveal and realize himself. Therefore our sins against the least of our fellow-men in the last resort concern God. Therefore when we retard the progress of mankind, we retard the revelation of the glory of God. Our universe is not a despotic monarchy, with God above the starry canopy and ourselves down here; it is a spiritual commonwealth with God in the midst of us.

We are on Christian ground when we insist on putting humanity into the picture. Jesus always deliberately and energetically bound man and God together. He would not let us deal with man apart from God, nor with God apart from man. We can not have forgiveness from God while we refuse forgiveness to any man. "What ye have done to these, ye have done to me; what ye have not done to these, ye have not done to me." This identification of the interests of God and man is characteristic of the religion of Jesus. Wherever God is isolated, we drop back to a pre-Christian stage of religion.

SIN IS SELFISHNESS

Sin is essentially selfishness. That definition is more in harmony with the social gospel than with an individualistic type of religion. The sinful mind, then, is the unsocial and antisocial mind. To find the climax of sin we must not linger over a man who swears, or sneers at religion, or denies the mystery of the Trinity, but put our hands on social groups who have turned the patrimony of a nation into the private property of a small class, or have left the peasant laborers cowed, degraded, demoralized, and without rights in the land. When we find such in history, or in present-day life, we shall know we have struck real rebellion against God on the higher levels of sin.

SIN AS CONTRASTED TO SOCIAL RIGHTEOUSNESS

We have defined sin. But we need more than definition. We need realization of its nature in order to secure the right religious attitude toward it.

Sin is always revealed by contrast to righteousness. We get an adequate intellectual measure of it and feel the proper hate and repugnance for it only when we see it as the terrible defeat and frustration of a great good which we love and desire.

A better and more Christian method of getting a religious realization of sin is to bring before our minds the positive ideals of social righteousness contained in the person of Christ and in the Kingdom of God, and see sin as the treasonable force which frustrates and wrecks these ideals and despoils the earth of their enjoyment. It is Christ who convicts the world of sin and not Adam. The spiritual perfection of Jesus consists in the fact that he was so simply and completely filled with the love of God and man that he gave himself to the task of the Kingdom of God without any reservation or backsliding. This is the true standard of holiness. The fact that a man is too respectable to get drunk or to swear is no proof of his righteousness. His moral and religious quality must be measured by the intelligence and single-heartedness with which he merges his will and life in the divine purpose of the Kingdom of God. By contrast, a man's sinfulness stands out in its true proportion, not when he is tripped up by ill-temper or side-steps into shame, but when he seeks to establish a private kingdom of self-service and is ready to thwart and defeat the progress of mankind toward peace, toward justice, or toward a fraternal organization of economic life, because that would diminish his political privileges, his unearned income, and his power over the working classes.

It follows that a clear realization of the nature of sin depends on a clear vision of the Kingdom of God. We can not properly feel and know the reign of organized wrong now prevailing unless we constantly see it over against the reign of organized righteousness. Where the religious conception of the Kingdom of God is wanting, men will be untrained and unfit to see or to estimate the social manifestations of sin.

THEOLOGY IS NOT BLAMELESS

It would be unfair to blame theology for the fact that our race is still submerged under despotic government, under war and militarism, under landlordism, and under predatory industry and finance. But we can justly blame it for the fact that the Christian Church even now has hardly any realization that these things are large-scale sins. We can blame it in part for the fact that when a Christian minister in our country speaks of these sins he is charged with forgetting the simple gospel of sin and salvation, and is in danger of losing his position. This comes of shelving the doctrine of the Kingdom of God, or juggling feeble substitutes into its place. Theology has not been a faithful steward of the truth entrusted to it. The social gospel is its accusing conscience.

THE GREATEST SINS ARE THESE

This is the chief significance of the social gospel for the doctrine of sin: it revives the vision of the Kingdom of God. When men see the actual world over against the religious ideal, they become conscious of its constitutional defects and wrongs. Those who do their thinking in the light of the Kingdom of God make less of heresy and private sins. They reserve their shudders for men who keep the liquor and vice trade alive against public intelligence and law; for interests that organize powerful lobbies to defeat tenement or factory legislation, or turn factory inspection into sham; for nations that are willing to set the world at war in order to win or protect colonial areas of trade or usurious profit from loans to weaker peoples; and for private interests which are willing to push a peaceful nation into war because the stock exchange has a panic at the rumor of peace. These seem the unforgivable sins, the great demonstrations of rebellious selfishness, wherever the social gospel has revived the faith of the Kingdom of God.

THE RELIGIOUS MIND AND SIN

The Christian consciousness of sin is the basis of all doctrines about sin. A serious and humble sense of sinfulness is part of a religious view of life. Our consciousness of sin deepens as our moral insight matures and becomes religious. When we think on the level of law or public opinion, we speak of crime, vice, bad habits, or defective character. When our mind is in the attitude of religion, we pray: "Create in me a clean heart, O God, and renew a right spirit within me." When a man is within the presence and consciousness of God, he sees himself and his past actions and present conditions in the most searching light and in eternal connections. To lack the consciousness of sin is a symptom of moral immaturity or of an effort to keep the shutters down and the light out. The most highly developed individuals, who have the power of interpreting life for others, and who have the clearest realization of possible perfection and the keenest hunger for righteousness, also commonly have the most poignant sense of their shortcomings.

WE ARE INVOLVED IN TRAGEDY

By our very nature we are involved in tragedy. In childhood and youth we have imperious instincts and desires to drive us, and little knowledge to guide and control us. We commit acts of sensuality, cruelty, or dishonor, which nothing can wipe from our memory. A child is drawn into harmful habits which lay the foundation for later failings, and which may trip the man again when his powers begin to fail in later life. How many men and women have rushed with the starry eyes of hope into relations which brought them defilement of soul and the perversion of their most intimate life, but from which they could never again extricate themselves by any wrench. "Forgive us our trespasses." "Lead us not into temptation." The weakness or the stubbornness of our will and the tempting situations of life combine to weave the tragic web of sin and failure of which we all make experience before we are through with our years.

THE SOCIAL GOSPEL MAKES THE INDIVIDUAL RESPONSIBLE FOR SIN

Any religious tendency or school of theology must be tested by the question whether it does justice to the religious consciousness of sin. Now, one cause of distrust against the social gospel is that its exponents often fail to show an adequate appreciation of the power and guilt of sin. Its teachings seem to put the blame for wrongdoing on the environment, and instead of stiffening and awakening the sense of responsibility in the individual, it teaches him to unload it on society.

There is doubtless truth in this accusation. The emphasis on environment and on the contributory guilt of the community does offer a chance to unload responsibility, and human nature is quick to seize the chance.

But the old theology has had its equivalents for environment. Men unloaded on original sin, on the devil, and on the decrees of God. Adam began soon after the Fall to shift the blame. This shiftiness seems to be one of the clearest and most universal effects of original sin.

A health officer of Toronto told me a story which illustrates the consciousness of sin created by the old religious teaching. If milk is found too dirty, the cans are emptied and marked with large red labels. This hits the farmer where he lives. He may not care about the health of Toronto, but he does care for the good opinion of his own neighborhood, and when he drives to the station and finds his friends chuckling over the red labels on his cans, it acts as a moral irritant. One day a Mennonite farmer found his cans labeled and he swore a worldly oath. The Mennonites are a devout people who take the teachings of Christ seriously and refuse to swear, even in law courts. This man was brought before his church and excluded. But, mark well, not for introducing cow-dung into the intestines of babies, but for expressing his belief in the damnation of the wicked in a nontheological way. When his church will hereafter have fully digested the social gospel, it may treat the case this way: "Our brother was angry and used the name of God profanely in his anger; we urge him to settle this alone with God. But he has also defiled the milk supply by unclean methods. Having the life and health of young children in his keeping, he has failed in his trust. Voted, that he be excluded until he has proved his lasting repentance." The result would be the same, but the sense of sin would do its work more intelligently.

SHIFTING THE EMPHASIS

It may well be that with some individuals there is a loss of seriousness in the sense of sin as a result of the social gospel. But on the whole the result consists chiefly in shifting the emphasis and assigning a new valuation to different classes of sins. Attention is concentrated on questions of public morality, on wrongs done by whole classes or professions of men, on sins which enervate and submerge entire mill towns or agricultural states. These sins have been side-stepped by the old theology. We now have to make up for a fatal failure in past teaching.

We feel a deep consciousness of sin when we realize that we have wasted our years, dissipated our energies, left our opportunities unused, frustrated the grace of God, and dwarfed and shamed the personality which God intended when he called us into life. It is a similar and even deeper misery to realize that our past life has hurt and blocked the Kingdom of God, the sum of all good, the essential aim of God himself. Our duty to the Kingdom of God is on a higher level than all other duties. To aid it is the supreme joy. To have failed it by our weakness, to have hampered it by our ignorance, to have resisted its prophets, to have contradicted its truths, to have denied it in time of danger, to have betrayed it for thirty pieces of silver—this is the most poignant consciousness of sin. The social gospel opens our eyes to the ways in which religious men do all these things. It plunges us in a new baptism of repentance.

THE TRANSMISSION OF SIN

How is sin transmitted from generation to generation? How is it made enduring and universal throughout the race?

This is by no means an academic question. Theology ought to be the science of redemption and offer scientific methods for the eradication of sin. In dealing with any epidemic disease, the first thing is to isolate the bacillus, and the second to see how it propagates and spreads. We must inquire for the lines of communication and contagion by which sin runs vertically down through history and horizontally through the strata of contemporary society.

THE TRUTH IN THE DOCTRINE OF ORIGINAL SIN

Theology has dealt with this problem in the doctrine of original sin. Many modern theologians are ready to abandon this doctrine, and among laymen it seems to carry so little sense of reality that audiences often smile at its mention. I take pleasure, therefore, in defending it. It is one of the few attempts of individualistic theology to get a solidaristic view of its field of work. This doctrine views the race as a great unity, descended from a single head, and knit together through all ages by unity of origin and blood. This natural unity is the basis and carrier for the transmission and universality of sin. Depravity of will and corruption of nature are transmitted wherever life itself is transmitted.

THE BIOLOGICAL ASPECTS OF ORIGINAL SIN

Science, to some extent, corroborates the doctrine of original sin. Evil does flow down the generations through the channels of biological coherence. Idiocy and feeblemindedness, neurotic disturbances, weakness of inhibition, perverse desires, stubbornness and antisocial impulses in children must have had their adequate biological causes somewhere back on the line, even if we lack the records.

Even in normal individuals the animal instincts preponderate over the spiritual motives and restraints. All who have to train the young find themselves marshaling motives and forces to strengthen the higher desires against the drag of unwillingness. "The spirit is willing, but the flesh is weak," is a formula of Jesus. Paul's description of the struggle of flesh and spirit in his life is a classical expression of the tragedies enacted in the intimate life of every one who has tried to make his recalcitrant ego climb the steep path of perfection: "The good which I would I do not; but the evil which I would not, that I practice."

According to orthodox theology, man's nature passed through a fatal debasement at the beginning of history. According to evolutionary science the impulses connected with our alimentary and reproductive organs run far back in the evolution of the race and are well established and imperious, whereas the social, altruistic, and spiritual impulses are of recent development and relatively weak. We can take our choice of the explanations. In either case a faulty equipment has come down to us through the reproductive life of the race.

DEFECTS IN THE DOCTRINE OF ORIGINAL SIN

There is, then, a substance of truth in this unpopular doctrine of original sin. But the old theology overworked it. It tried to involve us in the guilt of Adam as well as in his debasement of nature and his punishment of death. It fixed on us all a uniform corruption, and made it so complete that all evil resulting from personal sins seems trivial and irrelevant. If our will is so completely depraved, where do we get the freedom on which alone responsibility can be based? If a child is by nature set on evil, hostile to God, and a child of the devil, what is the use of education? For education presupposes an appetite for good which only needs awakening, direction, and spiritual support.

THE SOCIAL HEREDITY OF SIN

Theology was right in emphasizing the biological transmission of evil on the basis of race solidarity, but it strained the back of the doctrine by overloading it. On the other hand, it slighted or overlooked the fact that sin is transmitted along the lines of social tradition. This channel is at least as important as the other and far more susceptible of religious influence and control. Original sin deals with dumb forces of nature; social tradition is ethical and may be affected by conscious social action. Only the lack of social information and orientation in the past can explain the fact that theology has made so little of this.

That sin is lodged in social customs and institutions and is absorbed by the individual from his social group is so plain that any person with common sense can observe it, but I have found only a few, even among the modern handbooks of theology, which show a clear recognition of the theological importance of this fact. The social gospel has from the first emphasized it, and our entire religious method of dealing with children, adolescents, students, industrial and professional groups, and neighborhoods, is being put on a different basis in consequence of this new insight. Systematic theology is not running even with practical theology at this point. A theology for the social gospel would have to say that original sin is partly social. It runs down the generations not only by biological propagation but also by social assimilation.

Theologians sometimes dispatch this matter easily as "the force of evil example." There is much more in it. We deal here not only with the instinct of imitation, but with the spiritual authority of society over its members.

In the main the individual takes over his moral judgments and valuations from his social class, profession, neighborhood, and nation, making only slight personal modifications in the group standards. Only earnest or irresponsible persons are likely to enter into any serious opposition or contradiction, and then often on a single matter only, which exhausts their power of opposition. The deep marks which such a struggle with our group, especially in youth, leaves on our memory show how hard it was at the time.

A group may be better or worse than a given member in it. It may require more neatness, fortitude, efficiency, and hard work than he is accustomed to. In that case the boy entering a good shop or a fine college fraternity is very promptly educated upward. On the other hand, if a group practices evil, it will excuse or idealize it, and resent any private judgment which condemns it. Evil then becomes part of the standards of morality sanctioned by the authority of society. This confuses the moral judgment of the individual. The faculty of inhibition goes wrong.

THE SOURCE OF AUTHORITY IN SIN

Theology has always been deeply interested in the problem of authority in religion. The problem of authority in sin is of equal importance. Religious faith in the individual would be weak and intermittent unless it could lean on permanent social authorities. Sin in the individual is shamefaced and cowardly except where society backs and protects it. This makes a decisive difference in the practical task of overcoming a given evil.

The case of alcoholic intoxication may serve as an example. Intoxication . . . is one of the universal marks of barbarism. In civilization it is a survival, and its phenomena become increasingly intolerable and disgusting to the scientific and to the moral mind. Nevertheless, alcoholic drinking customs have prevailed and still prevail throughout civilization. What has given the practice of injecting a seductive drug into the human organism so enduring a hold? Other drug habits, such as the opium, cocaine, or heroin habits, are secretive and ashamed. Why does the alcohol habit flourish in the open? Aside from the question of the economic forces behind it . . . the difference is due to social authority.

The idealization of evil is an indispensable means for its perpetuation and transmission. But the most potent motive for its protection is its profitableness. Ordinarily sin is an act of weakness and side-stepping, followed by shame the next day. But when it is the source of prolific income, it is no longer a shamefaced vagabond slinking through the dark, but an army with banners, entrenched and defiant. The bigger the dividends, the stiffer the resistance against anything that would cut them down. When fed with money, sin grows wings and claws.

THE SOCIAL TRANSMISSION OF SIN

The theological doctrine of original sin is an important effort to see sin in its totality and to explain its unbroken transmission and perpetuation. But this explanation of the facts is very fragmentary, and theology has done considerable harm in concentrating the attention of religious minds on the biological transmission of evil. It has diverted our minds from the power of social transmission, from the authority of the social group in justifying, urging, and idealizing wrong, and from the decisive influence of economic profit in the defense and propagation of evil. These are ethical facts, but they have the greatest religious importance, and they have just as much right to being discussed in theology as the physical propagation of the species, or creationism and traducianism. There is the more inducement to teach clearly on the social transmission and perpetuation of sin because the ethical and religious forces can really do something to check and prevent the transmission of sin along social channels, whereas the biological transmission of original sin, except for the possible influence of eugenics, seems to be beyond our influence.

We need only mention some of the groups in our own national social life to realize how they vary in moral quality and how potent they are by virtue of their collective life: high school fraternities; any college community; a trade union; . . . any military organization; an officers' corps; the police force; the inside group of a local political party; the Free Masons; the Grange; the legal profession; a conspiracy like the Black Hand.

These super-personal forces count in the moral world not only through their authority over their members, but through their influence in the general social life. They front the world outside of them. Their real object usually lies outside. The assimilative power they exert over their members is only their form of discipline by which they bring their collective body into smooth and efficient working order. They are the most powerful ethical forces in our communities.

Evil collective forces have usually fallen from a better estate. Organizations are rarely formed for avowedly evil ends. They drift into evil under sinister leadership, or under the pressure of need or temptation. For instance, a small corrupt group in a city council, in order to secure control, tempts the weak, conciliates and serves good men, and turns the council itself into a force of evil in the city; an inside ring in the police force grafts on the vice trade, and draws a part of the force into protecting crime and browbeating decent citizens; a trade union fights for the right to organize a shop, but resorts to violence and terrorizing; a trust, desiring to steady prices and to get away from antiquated competition, undersells the independents and evades or purchases legislation. This tendency to deterioration shows the soundness of the social instincts, but also the ease with which they go astray, and the need of righteous social institutions to prevent temptation.

THE EVIL THAT MEN DO LIVES AFTER THEM

In some of our swampy forests the growth of ages has produced impenetrable thickets of trees and undergrowth, woven together by creepers, and inhabited by things that creep or fly. Every season sends forth new growth under the urge of life, but always developing from the old growth and its seeds, and still perpetuating the same rank mass of life.

The life of humanity is infinitely interwoven, always renewing itself, yet always perpetuating what has been. The evils of one generation are caused by the wrongs of the generations that preceded, and will in turn condition the sufferings and temptations of those who come after. Our Italian immigrants are what they are because the Church and the land system of Italy have made them so. The Mexican peon is ridden by the Spanish past. Capitalistic Europe has fastened its yoke on the neck of Africa. When Negroes are hunted from a northern city like beasts, or when a southern city degrades the whole nation by turning the savage inhumanity of a mob into a public festivity, we are continuing to sin because our fathers created the conditions of sin by the African slave trade and by the unearned wealth they gathered from slave labor for generations.

Stupid dynasties go on reigning by right of the long time they have reigned. The laws of the ancient Roman despotism were foisted by ambitious lawyers on medieval communities, to which they were in no wise fitted, and once more strangled liberty, and dragged free farmers into serfdom. When once the common land of a nation, and its mines and waters, have become the private property of a privileged band, nothing short of a social earthquake can pry them from their right of collecting private taxes. Superstitions which originated in the third century are still faithfully cultivated by great churches, compressing the minds of the young with fear, and cherished by the old as their most precious faith. Ideas struck out by a wrestling mind in the heat of an argument are erected by later times into proof-texts more decisive than masses of living facts. One nation arms because it fears another; the other arms more because this armament alarms it; each subsidizes a third and a fourth to aid it. Two fight; all fight; none knows how to stop; a planet is stained red in a solidarity of hate and horror.

FALSE CONCEPTIONS OF THE KINGDOM OF EVIL

Popular superstition, systematized and reinforced by theology, and inculcated by all the teaching authority of the medieval Church, built up an overwhelming impression of the power of evil. The Christian spirit was thrown into an attitude of defense only. The best that could be done was to hold the powers of darkness at bay by the sign of the cross, by holy water, by sacred amulets, by prayer, by naming holy names. The church buildings and church yards were places of refuge from which the evil spirits were banned. The gargoyles of Gothic architecture are the evil spirits escaping from the church buildings because the spiritual power within is unbearable to them.

The belief in a demonic kingdom was in no wise attacked in the Reformation. Luther's sturdy belief in devils is well known. Indeed, the belief which had been built up for centuries by the Church, came to its terrible climax during the age of the Reformation in the witch trials. From A.D. 1400 to 1700, hundreds of thousands of women and girls were imprisoned, tortured, and burned. These witch trials were grounded on the belief in the satanic kingdom. Thomas Aquinas furnished the theological basis; the Inquisition reduced it to practice; Innocent VIII in 1484 in the bull *Summis desiderantes* lent it the highest authority of the Church; the *Malleus Maleficarum* (1487 or 1488) codified it; lawyers, judges, informers, and executioners exploited it for gain; information given by malice, fear, or the shrieks of the tortured made the contagion self-perpetuating and ever spreading. It prevailed in Protestant countries equally with Catholic. To believe in the machinations of evil spirits and their compact with witches was part of orthodoxy, part of profounder piety. Even if the devil and his spirits are not real but a figment of imagination, yet at that time the devil was real, just as real as any flesh and blood being and far more efficient. Theology had made him real. The Reformation theology did not end this craze of horror. Aside from the humane religious spirit of a few who wrote against it, it was the blessed skepticism of the age of enlightenment and the dawn of modern science which saved humanity from the furies of a theology which had gone wrong.

THE PASSING OF BELIEF IN EVIL SPIRITS

Today the belief in a satanic kingdom exists only where a religious and theological tradition keeps it alive. It is not spontaneous, and it would not originate anew. Its lack of vitality is proved by the fact that even those who accept the existence of a personal Satan without question are not influenced in their daily life by the practical belief in evil spirits. The demons have faded away into poetical unreality. Satan alone remains, but he has become a literary and theological devil, and most often a figure of speech. He is a theological necessity rather than a religious reality. He is needed to explain the Fall and the Temptation, and he reappears in eschatology. But our most orthodox theology on this point would have seemed cold and skeptical to any of the great theologians of the past.

THE POWER AND REALITY OF EVIL REMAIN

Yet we ought to get a solidaristic and organic conception of the power and reality of evil in the world. If we miss that, we shall see only disjointed facts. The social gospel is the only influence which can renew the idea of the kingdom of evil in modern minds, because it alone has an adequate sense of solidarity and a sufficient grasp of the historical and social realities of sin. In this modern form the conception would offer religious values similar to those of the old idea, but would not make such drafts on our credulity, and would not invite such unchristian superstitions and phantasms of fear.

THE SIN OF ALL IS IN EACH

The doctrine of original sin was meant to bring us all under the sense of guilt. Theology in the past has labored to show that we are in some sense partakers of Adam's guilt. But the conscience of mankind has never been convinced. Partakers in his wretchedness we might well be by our family coherence, but guilt belongs only to personality, and requires will and freedom. On the other hand, an enlightened conscience can not help feeling a growing sense of responsibility and guilt for the common sins under which humanity is bound and to which we all contribute.

At the close of his great invective against the religious leaders of his nation, Jesus has a solidaristic vision of the spiritual unity of the generations. He warns his contemporaries that by doing over again the acts of their forefathers, they will bring upon them not only the blood they shed themselves, but the righteous blood shed long before. By solidarity of action and spirit we enter into solidarity of guilt. This applies to our spiritual unity with our contemporaries. If in the most restricted sphere of life we act on the same sinful principles of greed and tyranny on which the great exploiters and despots act, we share their guilt. If we consent to the working principles of the kingdom of evil, and do not counteract it with all our strength, but perhaps even fail to see its ruinous evil, then we are part of it and the salvation of Christ has not yet set us free.

⁂ 5 ⁂

Salvation: Personal and Social

PERSONAL SALVATION IS IMPORTANT

If our exposition of the super-personal agents of sin and of the kingdom of evil is true, then evidently a salvation confined to the soul and its personal interests is an imperfect and only partly effective salvation.

Yet the salvation of the individual is, of course, an essential part of salvation. Every new being is a new problem of salvation. It is always a great and wonderful thing when a young spirit enters into voluntary obedience to God and feels the higher freedom with which Christ makes us free. It is one of the miracles of life. The burden of the individual is as heavy now as ever. The consciousness of wrongdoing, of imperfection, of a wasted life lies on many and they need forgiveness and strength for a new beginning. Modern pessimism drains the finer minds of their confidence in the world and the value of life itself. At present we gasp for air in a crushing and monstrous world. Any return of faith is an experience of salvation.

Therefore our discussion can not pass personal salvation by. We might possibly begin where the old gospel leaves off, and ask our readers to take all the familiar experiences and truths of personal evangelism and religious nurture for granted in what follows. But our understanding of personal salvation itself is deeply affected by the new solidaristic comprehension furnished by the social gospel.

The social gospel furnishes new tests for religious experience. We are not disposed to accept the converted souls whom the individualistic evangelism supplies, without looking them over. Some who have been saved and perhaps reconsecrated a number of times are worth no more to the Kingdom of God than they were before. Some become worse through their revival experiences, more self-righteous, more opinionated, more steeped in unrealities and stupid over against the most important things, more devoted to emotions and unresponsive to real duties. We have the highest authority for the fact that men may grow worse by getting religion.

THE TRUE MEANING OF SALVATION

When we undertook to define the nature of sin, we accepted the old definition that sin is selfishness and rebellion against God, but we insisted on putting humanity into the picture. The definition of sin as selfishness gets its reality and nipping force only when we see humanity as a great solidarity and God indwelling in it. In the same way the terms and definitions of salvation get more realistic significance and ethical reach when we see the internal crises of the individual in connection with the social forces that play upon him or go out from him. The form which the process of redemption takes in a given personality will be determined by the historical and social spiritual environment of the man. At any rate any religious experience in which our fellow-men have no part or thought does not seem to be a distinctively Christian experience.

If sin is selfishness, salvation must be a change which turns a man from self to God and humanity. His sinfulness consisted in a selfish attitude, in which he was at the center of the universe, and God and all his fellow-men were means to serve his pleasures, increase his wealth, and set off his egotisms. Complete salvation, therefore, would consist in an attitude of love in which he would freely co-ordinate his life with the life of his fellows in obedience to the loving impulses of the spirit of God, thus taking his part in a divine organism of mutual service. When a man is in a state of sin, he may be willing to harm the life and lower the self-respect of a woman for the sake of his desires; he may be willing to take some of the mental and spiritual values out of the life of a thousand families, and lower the human level of a whole mill-town in order to increase his own dividend or maintain his autocratic sense of power. If this man came under the influence of the mind of Christ, he would see men and women as children of God with divine worth and beauty, and this realization would cool his lust or covetousness. Living now in the consciousness of the pervading spiritual life of God, he would realize that all his gifts and resources are a loan of God for higher ends, and would do his work with greater simplicity of mind and brotherliness.

Of course in actual life there is no complete Christian transformation. It takes an awakened and regenerated mind a long time to find itself intellectually and discover what life henceforth is to mean to him, and his capacity for putting into practice what he knows he wants to do, will be something like the capacity of an untrained hand to express artistic imaginations. But in some germinal and rudimentary form salvation must turn us from a life centered on ourselves toward a life going out toward God and men. God is the all-embracing source and exponent of the common life and good of mankind. When we submit to God, we submit to the supremacy of the common good. Salvation is the voluntary socializing of the soul.

CONVERSION A BREAK WITH THE PAST AND THE GROUP

Conversion has usually been conceived as a break with our sinful past. But in many cases it is also a break with the sinful past of a social group. Suppose a boy has been joining in cruel or lustful actions because his gang regards such things as fine and manly. If later he breaks with such actions, he will not only have to wrestle with his own habits, but with the social attractiveness and influence of his little humanity. If a workingman becomes an abstainer, he will find out that intolerance is not confined to the good. In primitive Christianity baptism stood for a conscious break with pagan society. This gave it a powerful spiritual reaction. Conversion is most valuable if it throws a revealing light not only across our own past, but across the social life of which we are part, and makes our repentance a vicarious sorrow for all. The prophets felt so about the sins of their nation. Jesus felt so about Jerusalem, and Paul about unbelieving Israel.

We call our religious crisis "conversion" when we think of our own active break with old habits and associations and our turning to a new life. Paul introduced the forensic term "justification" into our religious vocabulary to express a changed legal status before God; his term "adoption" expresses the same change in terms derived from family life. We call the change "regeneration" when we think of it as an act of God within us, creating a new life.

DEEP RELIGIOUS EXPERIENCES ARE SOCIAL

In the Bible we have several accounts of religious experiences which were fundamental in the life of its greatest characters. A few are told in their own striking phrases. Others are described by later writers, and in that case indicate what popular opinion expected such men to experience. Now, none of these experiences, so far as I see, are of that solitary hope in which a soul struggles for its own salvation in order to escape the penalties of sin or to attain perfection and peace for itself. All were experienced with a conscious outlook toward humanity. When Moses saw the glory of God in the flaming bush and learned the ineffable name of the Eternal, it was not the salvation of Moses which was in question but the salvation of his people from the bondage of Egypt. When young Samuel first heard the call of the voice in the darkness, it spoke to him of priestly extortion and the troubled future of his people. When Isaiah saw the glory of the Lord above the Cherubim, he realized by contrast that he was a man of unclean lips, but also that he dwelt among a people of unclean lips. His cleansing and the dedication which followed were his preparation for taking hold of the social situation of his nation. In Jeremiah we are supposed to have the attainment of the religion of the individual, but even his intimate experiences were all in full view of the fate of his nation. Paul's experience at Damascus was the culmination of his personal struggle and his emergence into spiritual freedom. But his crisis got its intensity from its social background. He was deciding, so far as he was concerned, between the old narrow nationalistic religion of conservative Judaism and a wider destiny for his people, between the validity of the law and spiritual liberty, between the exclusive claims of Israel on the Messianic hope and a world-wide participation in the historical prerogatives of the first-born people.

We can not afford to rate this group of religious experiences at a low value. As with us all, the theology of the prophets was based on their personal experiences. Out of them grew their ethical monotheism and their

God-consciousness. This was the highest element in the spiritual heritage of his people which came to Jesus. He reinterpreted and perfected it in his personality, and in that form it has remained the highest factor among the various historical strains combined in our religion.

These prophetic experiences were not superficial. There was soul-shaking emotion, a deep sense of sin, faith in God, longing for him, self-surrender, enduement with spiritual power. Yet they were not ascetic, not individualistic, not directed toward a future life. They were social, political, solidaristic.

The saint of the future will need not only a theocentric mysticism which enables him to realize God, but an anthropocentric mysticism which enables him to realize his fellow-men in God. The more we approach pure Christianity, the more will the Christian signify a man who loves mankind with a religious passion and excludes none. The feeling which Jesus had when he said, "I am the hungry, the naked, the lonely," will be in the emotional consciousness of all holy men in the coming days. The sense of solidarity is one of the distinctive marks of the true followers of Jesus.

THE SALVATION OF SUPER-PERSONAL FORCES

Super-personal forces are saved when they come under the law of Christ. A State which uses its terrible power of coercion to smite and crush offenders as a protection to the rest is still under brutal law. A State which deals with those who have erred in the way of teaching, discipline, and restoration has come under the law of Christ and is to that extent a saved community. "By their fruits ye shall know them." States are known by their courts and prisons and contract labor systems, or by their juvenile courts and parole systems. A change in penology may be an evidence of salvation.

A State which uses its superior power to overrun a weaker neighbor by force, or to wrest a valuable right of way from it by instigating a *coup d'état*, or uses intimidation to secure mining or railway concessions or to force a loan at various rates on a half-civilized State, is in mortal sin. A State which asks only for an open door and keeps its own door open in return, and which speaks as courteously to a backward State as to one with a big fleet, is to that extent a Christian community.

With composite personalities as with individuals "the love of money is the root of all evil." Communities and nations fall into wild fits of anger and cruelty; they are vain and contemptuous of others; they lie and love lies; they sin against their critical conscience; they fall in love with virile and magnetic men just as women do. These are the temptations and dangers which every democracy will meet and from which it will recover with loss and some shame. But, as has been said before, evils become bold and permanent when there is money in them. It was the need of protecting wealth against poverty which made the courts and the criminal law so cruel in the past. It was theological superstition which started the epidemic of witch trials in Europe, but it was the large fees that fell to the lawyers and informers which made that craze so enduring. Nearly all modern wars have had their origin in the covetousness of trade and finance.

The salvation of the super-personal beings is by coming under the law of Christ. The fundamental step of repentance and conversion for professions and organizations is to give up monopoly power and the incomes derived from legalized extortion, and to come under the law of service, content with a fair income for honest work. The corresponding step in the case of governments and political oligarchies, both in monarchies and in capitalistic semi-democracies, is to submit to real democracy. Therewith they step out of the kingdom of evil into the Kingdom of God.

❧ 6 ❧

Religion and Social Reform

JESUS WAS NOT A SOCIAL REFORMER

But in truth Jesus was not a social reformer of the modern type. Sociology and political economy were just as far outside of his range of thought as organic chemistry or the geography of America. He saw the evil in the life of men and their sufferings, but he approached these facts purely from the moral, and not from the economic or historical point of view. He wanted men to live a right life in common, and only in so far as the social questions are moral questions did he deal with them as they confronted him.

RELIGION THE SOURCE OF HIS POWER

And he was more than a teacher of morality. Jesus had learned the greatest and deepest and rarest secret of all—how to live a religious life. When the question of economic wants is solved for the individual and all his outward adjustments are as comfortable as possible, he may still be haunted by the horrible emptiness of his life and feel that existence is a meaningless riddle and delusion. If the question of the distribution of wealth were solved for all society and all lived in average comfort and without urgent anxiety, the question would still be how many would be at peace with their own souls and have that enduring joy and contentment which alone can make the outward things fair and sweet and rise victorious over change. Universal prosperity would not be incompatible with universal ennui and *Weltschmerz.* Beyond the question of economic distribution lies the question of moral relations; and beyond the moral relations to men lies the question of the religious communion with that spiritual reality in which we live and move and have our deepest being—with God, the Father of our spirits. Jesus had realized the life of God in the soul of man and the life of man in the love of God. That was the real secret of his life, the wellspring of his purity, his compassion, his unwearied courage, his unquenchable idealism; he knew the Father. But if he had that greatest of all possessions, the real key to the secret of life, it was his highest social duty to share it and help others to gain what he had. He had to teach men to live as children in the presence of their Father, and no longer as slaves cringing before a despot. He had to show them that the ordinary life of selfishness and hate and anxiety and chafing ambition and covetousness is no life at all, and that they must enter into a new world of love and solidarity and inward contentment. There was no service that he could render to men which would equal that.

All other help lay in concentric circles about that redemption of the spirit and flowed out from it.

No comprehension of Jesus is even approximately true which fails to understand that the heart of his heart was religion. No man is a follower of Jesus in the full sense who has not through him entered into the same life with God. But on the other hand no man shares his life with God whose religion does not flow out, naturally and without effort, into all relations of his life and reconstruct everything that it touches. Whoever uncouples the religious and the social has not understood Jesus. Whoever sets any bounds for the reconstructive power of the religious life over the social relations and institutions of men, to that extent denies the faith of the Master.

JESUS DEALT WITH CONCRETE ISSUES

If we want to understand the real aims of Jesus, we must watch him in his relation to his own times. He was not a timeless religious teacher, philosophizing vaguely on human generalities. He spoke for his own age, about concrete conditions, responding to the stirrings of the life that surged about him. We must follow him in his adjustment to the tendencies of the time, in his affinity for some men and his repulsion of others. That is the method by which we classify and locate a modern thinker or statesman.

The Christian movement began with John the Baptist. All the evangelists so understood it. John himself accepted Jesus as the one who was to continue and consummate his own work. Jesus linked John closely to himself. He paid tribute to the rugged bravery and power of the man, and asserted that the new religious era had begun with John as an era of strenuous movement and stir. "The law and the prophets were until John; from that time the gospel of the Kingdom of God is preached, and every man entereth violently into it." *

Both Jesus and the people generally felt that in John they had an incarnation of the spirit of the ancient prophets. He wore their austere garb; he shared their utter fearlessness, their ringing directness of speech, their consciousness of speaking an inward message of God. The substance of his message was also the same. It was the old prophetic demand for ethical obedience. He and his disciples fasted and he taught them certain forms of prayer, but in his recorded teaching to the people there is not a word about the customary ritual of religion, about increased Sabbath observance, about stricter washings and sacrifices, or the ordinary exercises of piety. He spoke only of repentance, of ceasing from wrongdoing. He hailed the professional exponents of religion who came to hear him, as a brood of snakes wriggling away from the flames of judgment. He demolished the self-confidence of the Jew and his pride of descent and religious monopoly, just as Amos or Jeremiah did. If God wanted children of Abraham, they were cheap and easy to get; God would turn the pebbles of the Jordan valley into children of Abraham by

* Luke 16:16.

the million. But what God wanted, and found hard to get, was men who would quit evil. Yet God was bound to get such and would destroy all others. Now was the time to repent and by the badge of baptism to enroll with the purified remnant.

The people asked for details. What would repentance involve? "What then must we do?" He replied: "He that hath two coats, let him share with him that hath none; and he that hath food, let him do likewise." The way to prepare for the Messianic era and to escape the wrath of the Messiah was to institute a brotherly life and to equalize social inequalities. If John thus conceived of the proper preparation for the Messianic salvation, how did he conceive of the Messianic era itself? Luke records his advice to two special classes of men, the taxgatherers and the soldiers. . . . John told them to stop being parasites and to live on their honest earnings.

SOCIAL WRONGS OBSTRUCT THE COMING OF THE KINGDOM

Would any preacher have defined repentance in these terms if his eyes had not been open to the social inequality about him and to the exploitation of the people by the representatives of organized society? Luke characterized John's purpose by quoting the call of Isaiah to make ready the way of the Lord by leveling down the hills and leveling up the valleys and making the crooked things straight. John would not have been so silent about the ordinary requirements of piety, and so terribly emphatic in demanding the abolition of social wrongs, if he had not felt that here were the real obstacles to the coming of the Kingdom of God. From this preaching, coupled with our general knowledge of the times, we can infer what his points of view and his hopes and expectations were, and also what was the real spring of the remarkable popular movement which he initiated. It was the national hope of Israel that carried the multitudes into the desert to hear John. The judgment which he proclaimed was not the individual judgment of later Christian theology, but the sifting of the Jewish people preparatory to establishing the renewed Jewish theocracy. The Kingdom of God which he announced as close at hand was the old hope of the people, and that embraced the restoration of the Davidic kingdom, the reign of social justice, and the triumph of the true religion. John was a true descendant of the prophets in denying that Jewish descent constituted a claim to share in the good time coming. He put the kingdom on an ethical basis. But it was still a social hope and it required social morality.

JESUS FOLLOWS IN THE FOOTSTEPS OF JOHN

Now Jesus accepted John as the forerunner of his own work. It was the popular movement created by John which brought Jesus out of the seclusion of Nazareth. He received John's baptism as the badge of the new Messianic hope and repentance. His contact with John and the events at the Jordan were evidently of decisive importance in the progress of his own inner life and his Messianic consciousness. When he left the Jordan the power of his own mission was upon him. He took up the formula of John: "The Kingdom of God has come nigh; repent!" He continued the same baptism. He drew his earliest and choicest disciples from the followers of John. When John was dead, some thought Jesus was John risen from the dead. He realized clearly the difference between the stern ascetic spirit of the Baptist and his own sunny trust and simple human love, but to the end of his life he championed John and dared the Pharisees to deny his divine mission. It seems impossible to assume that his own fundamental purpose, at least in the beginning of his ministry, was wholly divergent from that of John. In the main he shared John's national and social hope. His aim too was the realization of the theocracy.

Moreover, in joining hands with John, Jesus clasped hands with the entire succession of the prophets with whom he classed John. Their words were his favorite quotations. Like them he disregarded or opposed the ceremonial elements of religion and insisted on the ethical. Like them he sided with the poor and oppressed. As Amos and Jeremiah foresaw the conflict of their people with the Assyrians and the Chaldeans, so Jesus foresaw his nation drifting toward the conflict with Rome, and like them he foretold disaster, the fall of the temple and of the Holy City. That prophetic type of religion which constituted the chief religious heritage of his nation had laid hold on Jesus, and he had laid hold of it and had appropriated its essential spirit. In the poise and calm of his mind and manner, and in the love of his heart, he was infinitely above them all. But the greatest of all prophets was still one of the prophets, and that large interest in the national and social life which had been inseparable from the religion of the prophets was part of his life too. The presumption is that Jesus shared the fundamental religious purpose of the prophets. If anyone asserts that he abandoned the collective hope and gave his faith solely to religious individualism, he will have to furnish express statements in which Jesus disavows the religious past of his people.

THE MEANING OF COMMUNITY

All these facts and sayings receive their real meaning when we think of them in connection with the Kingdom of God, the ideal human society to be established. Instead of a society resting on coercion, exploitation, and inequality, Jesus desired to found a society resting on love, service, and equality. These new principles were so much the essence of his character and of his view of life, that he lived them out spontaneously and taught them in everything that he touched in his conversation or public addresses. God is a father; men are neighbors and brothers; let them act accordingly. Let them love, and then life will be true and good. Let them seek the kingdom, and all things would follow.... If an individual or a class was outside of fraternal relations, he set himself to heal the breach. The Kingdom of God is the true human society; the ethics of Jesus taught the true social conduct which would create the true society. This would be Christ's test for any custom, law, or institution: does it draw men together or divide them?

PERSONAL AND SOCIAL REGENERATION NEEDED

In personal religion the first requirement is to repent and believe in the gospel. As long as a man is self-righteous and complacently satisfied with his moral attainments, there is no hope that he will enter into the higher development, and unless he has faith that a higher level of spiritual life is attainable, he will be lethargic and stationary.

Social religion, too, demands repentance and faith: repentance for our social sins; faith in the possibility of a new social order. As long as a man sees in our present society only a few inevitable abuses and recognizes no sin and evil deep-seated in the very constitution of the present order, he is still in a state of moral blindness and without conviction of sin. . . . Regeneration means that a man must pass under the domination of the spirit of Christ, so that he will judge of life as Christ would judge of it. That means a revaluation of social values. Things that are now "exalted among men" must become an abomination to him because they are built on wrong and misery. Unless a man finds his judgment at least on some fundamental questions in opposition to the current ideas of the age, he is still a child of this world and has not tasted the powers of the coming age. He will have to repent and believe if he wants to be a Christian in the full sense of the word.

No man can help the people until he is himself free from the spell which the present order has cast over our moral judgment. We have repeatedly pointed out that every social institution weaves a protecting integument of glossy idealization about itself like a colony of tent caterpillars in an apple tree. For instance, wherever militarism rules, war is idealized by monuments and paintings, poetry and song. The stench of the hospitals and the maggots of the battlefield are passed in silence, and the imagination of the people is filled with waving plumes and the shout of charging columns. A Russian general thought Verestchagin's pictures ought to be destroyed because they disenchanted the people. If war is ever to be relegated to the limbo of outgrown barbarism, we must shake off its magic. When we comprehend how few wars have ever been fought for the sake of justice or the people; how personal spite, the ambition of military professionals, the protection of capitalistic ventures are the real moving powers; how the governing classes pour out the blood and wealth of nations for private ends and exude patriotic enthusiasm like a squid secreting ink to hide its retreat—then the mythology of war will no longer bring us to our knees, and we shall fail to get drunk with the rest when martial intoxication sweeps the people off their feet.

THE DUTY OF THE RELIGIOUS MAN

The greatest contribution which any man can make to the social movement is the contribution of a regenerated personality, of a will which sets justice above policy and profit, and of an intellect emancipated from falsehood. Such a man will in some measure incarnate the principles of a higher social order in his attitude to all questions and in all his relations to men, and will be a wellspring of regenerating influences. If he speaks, his judgment will be a corrective force. If he listens, he will encourage the truth-teller and discourage the peddler of adulterated facts and maxims. If others lose heart, he will stay them with his inspired patience. If any new principle is to gain power in human history, it must take shape and life in individuals who have faith in it. The men of faith are the living spirits, the channels by which new truth and power from God enter humanity. To repent of our collective social sins, to have faith in the possibility and reality of a divine life in humanity, to submit the will to the purposes of the Kingdom of God, to permit the divine inspiration to emancipate and clarify the moral insight—this is the most intimate duty of the religious man who would help to build the coming Messianic era of mankind.

The fundamental contribution of every man is the change of his own personality. We must repent of the sins of existing society, cast off the spell of the lies protecting our social wrongs, have faith in a higher social order, and realize in ourselves a new type of Christian manhood which seeks to overcome the evil in the present world, not by withdrawing from the world, but by revolutionizing it.

If this new type of religious character multiplies among the young men and women, they will change the world when they come to hold the controlling positions of society in their maturer years. They will give a new force to righteous and enlightened public opinion, and will apply the religious sense of duty and service to the common daily life with a new motive and directness.

LOVE FOR GOD DEMANDS LOVE FOR MEN

Men tell us that religion ought to have an ethical outcome and that love of God is inseparable from love to men. They say it as if that were a new discovery. It ought to be a truism by this time. It was once the passionate message of the Hebrew prophets, and was embodied in the Christian religion as one of its axiomatic doctrines. "Whosoever doeth not righteousness is not of God, neither he that loveth not his brother. For this is the message which ye heard from the beginning, that we should love one another." These words were meant to repudiate the claim to Christian standing of any man whose religion was not ground deep in active and passionate good will toward men.

Moreover, in Christianity love must mean more than mild benevolence of feeling. Love gets its Christian definition from the personality of Jesus and from his death: "Hereby have we come to a comprehension of love, by the fact that he laid down his life for us; and we ought to lay down our life for the brethren. But whoso hath the world's goods, and beholdeth his brother in need, and shutteth up his compassion from him, now doth the love of God abide in him?" This passage shows how swiftly a Christian mind passed from the nature of love as defined by the death of Christ to social action in matters of property relations.

Thus the insistence that love to God must have its immediate result and counterpoise in love for men is one of the rudiments of Christian faith and feeling. But that does not exhaust the relations between the love of God and the love of man. The casual relation runs the other way too.

LOVE FOR MEN TRAINS THE LOVE FOR GOD

It is by loving men that we enter into a living love for God. Social work may be a gateway to conscious religion.

An actual love for God is a commonplace in religious talk, but it is not a common thing in fact. Aristotle questioned if such high feeling were possible. To have a strong sense of desire and joy and fellowship going out toward that great, unseen, intangible Power which fills the universe is nothing slight, but the highest attainment in the evolution of character, the fragrant blossoming of our spiritual nature.

We assume that love to God must come first and is the proper starting point and foundation for the love of man. Is it not just as much the other way? The love of man is our concrete object lesson in the kindergarten of love, and if we learn that well, and as fast as we learn that well, the love of God grows in us, and we become religious. This is biblical doctrine. "He that loveth not his brother whom he hath seen, how can he love God whom he hath not seen?" He that will not learn the multiplication tables which are easy, how can he comprehend algebra which is hard? No man hath beheld God at any time. "If we love one another, God abideth in us and his love is perfected in us." In other words, God is invisible and inaccessible in himself, but if we love one another, we make a place for him in our own life and will realize him and his love.

To love men, then, is an avenue to the living experience of God. There may be other paths that lead to him, such as the solitary search for truth, or the lonely way of mystic contemplation. But love is the surest way with fewest pitfalls, the broad way open to all sorts and conditions of men, and the way consecrated by Jesus Christ. We should expect, therefore, that those who are engaged in social work with a really loving spirit will find religion growing in them. If their religion in the past has been merely formal, it ought to grow warm and living. If it has been in the immature stage of dogmatism and ritualism, it ought to come to freedom and maturity. We might even look in social work for that most difficult triumph in the breeding of religion, the restoration of conscious religion where it was dead.

THE RELIGIOUS SOUL IS MASTER

Religion has the master word in human life. When patriotism, poetry, science, or philosophy rises to its highest level, it becomes religious. In the great moments of life, either in joy or sorrow, nothing suffices except religion.

Nearly all forms of charity and human betterment began in the souls of men and women who had the substance of religion in them. Their impulses of mercy or anger may have been uninstructed, but at least they saw and struck out before science or government moved. Living religion gives prophetic insight and daring, and so raises up the pioneers of love and justice. Other things being equal, a man of religious faith and temper is always the wiser and stronger. The religious souls are the master souls.

RELIGION AND ETHICS INSEPARABLE

Every forward step in the historical evolution of religion has been marked by a closer union of religion and ethics and by the elimination of nonethical religious performances. This union of religion and ethics reached its highest perfection in the life and mind of Jesus. After him Christianity quickly dropped back to the pre-Christian stage. Ceremonial actions and orthodox beliefs became indispensable to salvation; they had a value of their own, quite apart from their bearing on conduct. Theology had the task of defending and inculcating these nonethical ingredients of religion, and that pulled theology down. It is clear that our Christianity is most Christian when religion and ethics are viewed as inseparable elements of the same single-minded and wholehearted life, in which the consciousness of God and the consciousness of humanity blend completely. Any new movement in theology which emphatically asserts the union of religion and ethics is likely to be a wholesome and Christianizing force in Christian thought.

The social gospel is of that nature. It plainly concentrates religious interest on the great ethical problems of social life. It scorns the tithing of mint, anise, and cummin, at which the Pharisees are still busy, and insists on getting down to the weightier matters of God's law, to justice and mercy. It ties up religion not only with duty, but with big duty that stirs the soul with religious feeling and throws it back on God for help. The nonethical practices and beliefs in historical Christianity nearly all center on the winning of heaven and immortality. On the other hand, the Kingdom of God can be established by nothing except righteous life and action.

☙ 7 ❧

The Hope of Redeeming Society

THERE IS HOPE

To anyone who knows the sluggishness of humanity to good, the impregnable intrenchments of vested wrongs, and the long reaches of time needed from one milestone of progress to the next, the task of setting up a Christian social order in this modern world of ours seems like a fair and futile dream. Yet in fact it is not one tithe as hopeless as when Jesus set out to do it. When he told his disciples, "Ye are the salt of the earth; ye are the light of the world," he expressed the consciousness of a great historic mission to the whole of humanity. Yet it was a Nazarene carpenter speaking to a group of Galilean peasants and fishermen. Under the circumstances at that time it was an utterance of the most daring faith—faith in himself, faith in them, faith in what he was putting into them, faith in faith. Jesus failed and was crucified, first his body by his enemies, and then his spirit by his friends; but that failure was so amazing a success that today it takes an effort on our part to realize that it required any faith on his part to inaugurate the Kingdom of God and to send out his apostolate.

Today, as Jesus looks out upon humanity, his spirit must leap to see the souls responsive to his call. They are sown broadcast through humanity, legions of them. The harvest-field is no longer deserted. All about us we hear the clang of the whetstone and the rush of blades through the grain and the shout of the reapers. With all our faults and our slothfulness we modern men in many ways are more on a level with the real mind of Jesus than any generation that has gone before. If that first apostolate was able to remove mountains by the power of faith, such an apostolate as Christ could now summon might change the face of the earth.

THE FUTURE BELONGS TO THE SOWER

The apostolate of a new age must do the work of the sower. When the sower goes forth to sow his seed, he goes with the certainty of partial failure and the knowledge that a long time of patience and of hazard will intervene before he can hope to see the result of his work and his venture. In sowing the truth a man may never see or trace the results. The more ideal his conceptions are, and the farther they move ahead of his time, the larger will be the percentage of apparent failure. But he can afford to wait. The powers of life are on his side. He is like a man who has scattered his seed and then goes off to sleep by night and work by day, and all the while his seed, by the inscrutable chemistry of life, lays hold of the ingredients of its environment and builds them up to its own growth. The mustard-seed becomes a tree. The leaven assimilates the meal by biological processes. The new life penetrates the old humanity and transforms it. Robert Owen was a sower. His co-operative communities failed. He was able to help only a small fraction of the workingmen of his day. But his moral enthusiasm and his ideas fertilized the finest and most self-sacrificing minds among the working classes. They cherished his ultimate hopes in private and worked for realizable ends in public. The Chartist movement was filled with his spirit. The most influential leaders of English unionism in its great period after the middle of the nineteenth century were Owenites. The Rochdale Pioneers were under his influence, and the great co-operative movement in England, an economic force of the first importance, grew in some measure out of the seed which Owen had scattered. Other men may own the present. The future belongs to the sower—provided he scatters seed and does not mistake the chaff for it which once was so essential to the seed and now is dead and useless.

WE SEEK THE UNATTAINABLE

In asking for faith in the possibility of a new social order, we ask for no Utopian delusion. We know well that there is no perfection for man in this life: there is only growth toward perfection. In personal religion we look with seasoned suspicion at any one who claims to be holy and perfect, yet we always tell men to become holy and to seek perfection. We make it a duty to seek what is unattainable. We have the same paradox in the perfectibility of society. We shall never have a perfect social life, yet we must seek it with faith. We shall never abolish suffering. There will always be death and the empty chair and heart. There will always be the agony of love unreturned. Women will long for children and never press baby lips to their breasts. Men will long for fame and miss it. Imperfect moral insight will work hurt in the best conceivable social order. The strong will always have the impulse to exert their strength, and no system can be devised which can keep them from crowding and jostling the weaker. Increased social refinement will bring increased sensitiveness to pain. An American may suffer as much distress through a social slight as a Russian peasant under the knout. At best there is always but an approximation to a perfect social order. The Kingdom of God is always but coming.

THE SEARCH IS REWARDING

But every approximation to it is worth while. Every step toward personal purity and peace, though it only makes the consciousness of imperfection more poignant, carries its own exceeding great reward, and everlasting pilgrimage toward the kingdom of God is better than contented stability in the tents of wickedness.

And sometimes the hot hope surges up that perhaps the long and slow climb may be ending. In the past the steps of our race toward progress have been short and feeble, and succeeded by long intervals of sloth and apathy. But is that necessarily to remain the rate of advance? In the intellectual life there has been an unprecedented leap forward during the last hundred years. Individually we are not more gifted than our grandfathers, but collectively we have wrought our more epoch-making discoveries and inventions in one century than the whole race in the untold centuries that have gone before. If the twentieth century could do for us in the control of social forces what the nineteenth did for us in the control of natural forces, our own grandchildren would live in a society that would be justified in regarding our present social life as semibarbarous. Since the Reformation began to free the mind and to direct the force of religion toward morality, there has been a perceptible increase of speed. Humanity is gaining in elasticity and capacity for change, and every gain in general intelligence, in organizing capacity, in physical and moral soundness, and especially in responsiveness to ideal motives, again increases the ability to advance without disastrous reactions. The swiftness of evolution in our own country proves the immense latent perfectibility in human nature.

If at this juncture we can rally sufficient religious faith and moral strength to snap the bonds of evil and turn the present unparalleled economic and intellectual resources of humanity to the harmonious development of a true social life, the generations yet unborn will mark this as that great day of the Lord for which the ages waited, and count us blessed for sharing in the apostolate that proclaimed it.

THE SOCIAL GOSPEL AND THE FUTURE OF THE RACE

The future development of the race should have a larger place in practical Christian teaching. The great ethical issues of the future lie in this field, and the mind of Christian men and women should be active there. If we cannot be guided by moral and spiritual thought, we shall be guided by bitter experience. . . . We have the amplest warrant for directing the prophetic thought of religious men toward the social and political future of humanity, for all eschatology derived from Hebrew sources dealt with these interests. A stronger emphasis on the future of the race will simply restore the genuinely Christian emphasis.

All Christian discussions of the past and the future must be religious, and filled with the consciousness of God in human affairs. God is in history. He has the initiative. Where others see blind forces working dumb agony, we must see moral will working toward redemption and education. A religious view of history involves a profound sense of the importance of moral issues in social life. Sin ruins, righteousness establishes, and love consolidates. In the last resort the issues of future history lie in the moral qualities and religious faith of nations. This is the substance of all Hebrew and Christian eschatology.

We need a restoration of the millennial hope, which the Catholic Church dropped out of eschatology. It was crude in its form but wholly right in its substance.

The duration of a thousand years is a guess and immaterial. All efforts to fix times and seasons are futile. But the ideal of a social life in which the law of Christ shall prevail, and in which its prevalence shall result in peace, justice, and a glorious blossoming of human life, is a Christian ideal. An outlook toward the future in which the spiritual life is saved and the economic life is left unsaved is both unchristian and stupid. . . . Our chief interest in any millennium is the desire for a social order in which the worth and freedom of every last human being will be honored and protected; in which the brotherhood of man will be expressed in the common possession of the economic resources of society; and in which the spiritual good of humanity will be set high above the private profit interests of all materialistic groups.

As to the way in which the Christian ideal of society is to come—we must shift from catastrophe to development. Since the first century the divine Logos has taught us the universality of law, and we must apply it to the development of the Kingdom of God. It is the untaught and pagan mind which sees God's presence only in miraculous and thundering action; the more Christian our intellect becomes, the more we see God in growth. By insisting on organic development we shall follow the lead of Jesus when, in his parables of the sower and of the seed growing secretly, he tried to educate his disciples away from catastrophe to an understanding of organic growth. We shall also be following the lead of the Fourth Gospel, which translated the terms of eschatology into the operation of present spiritual forces. We shall be following the lead of the Church in bringing the future hope down from the clouds and identifying it with the Church; except that we do not confine it to the single institution of the Church, but see the coming of the Kingdom of God in all ethical and spiritual progress of mankind. To convert the catastrophic terminology of eschatology into developmental terms is another way of expressing faith in the immanence of God and in the presence of Christ. It is more religious to believe in a present than in an absent and future Christ. Jesus saw the Kingdom as present and future. This change from catastrophe to development is the most essential step to enable modern men to appreciate the Christian hope.

This process will have to utilize all constructive and educational forces in humanity. In our conception of personal regeneration, likewise, we have been compelled to think less of emotional crises and more of religious nurture and education. The coming of the Kingdom of God will be the regeneration of the super-personal life of the race, and will work out a social expression of what was contained in the personality of Christ.

The coming of the Kingdom of God will not be by peaceful development only, but by conflict with the kingdom of evil. We should estimate the power of sin too lightly if we forecast a smooth road. Nor does the insistence on continuous development eliminate the possibility and value of catastrophes. Political and social revolutions may shake down the fortifications of the kingdom of evil in a day. The Great War is a catastrophic stage in the coming of the Kingdom of God. Its direct effects will operate for generations. Our descendants will have a better perspective than we to see how all the sins of modern civilization have brought forth death after their own kind, and how the social repentance of nations may lay the foundation for a new beginning.

An eschatology which is expressed in terms of historic development has no final consummation. Its consummations are always the basis for further development. The Kingdom of God is always coming, but we can never say "Lo, here." Theologians often assert that this would be unsatisfactory. A kingdom of social righteousness can never be perfect; man remains flesh; new generations would have to be trained anew; only by a world catastrophe can the kingdom of glory be realized. Apparently we have to postulate a static condition in order to give our minds a rest; an endless perspective of development is too taxing. Fortunately God is not tired as easily as we. If we called humanity to a halt in a kingdom of glory, he would have on his hands some millions of eager spirits whom he has himself trained to ceaseless aspiration and achievement, and they would be dying of ennui. Besides, what is the use of a perfect ideal which never happens? A progressive kingdom of righteousness happens all the time in installments, like our own sanctification. Our race will come to an end in due time; the astronomical clock is already ticking which will ring in the end. Meanwhile we are on the march toward the Kingdom of God, and getting our reward by every fractional realization of it which makes us hungry for more. A stationary humanity would be a dead humanity. The life of the race is in its growth.

WHEN OUR WORK IS DONE

The day comes for each of us when our work is done and we are gathered to our fathers, and a man's soul must be calloused indeed if he is indifferent to the verdict that his fellow-men will pass on him after he is gone. Our selfish lusts may be hot in us while they last, but when all is done, we want to be remembered in love for some good we have done, for some enduring help we have given to mankind. It might well break a man's heart to know that posterity will class him forever, not with the friends of man who range about Jesus Christ as their leader, but with the oppressors and exploiters of the poor.

In so far as they have aided in the application of science to the production of wealth and in the perfecting of industrial organization, our captains of industry have had a great part in the permanent achievements of our age. The names of some of them who have made epoch-making advances in the broader organization of industry may be cited to students in centuries to come as marking the climax of capitalism and the unconscious transition to a new social order. But in so far as rich men have been mere accumulators of unearned wealth, they need expect no praise from the future. There is nothing in ethics, in politics, or in economics that makes the swollen fortunes of our day desirable or admirable. The indirect good done through them might have been accomplished in more direct ways. Their evil results will gather force far into the future. The deadliness of sin is never sized up in one generation. Sin is always pregnant with Death, but it takes time to bring her terrible child to birth. From now on the great problem of statesmanship in the capitalistic nations will be how to stop the further accumulation of unearned wealth; how to dissipate the present great fortunes without causing a revolution; how to make way for human progress in spite of their obstructive influence; in short, how to undo what the profit makers have labored to do. Men hereafter will differ whether the great capitalists have done more good by their management or more harm by their accumulations. Before God they will have to answer for the fact that the main purpose of their industrial work was not social achievement, but private profit.

THE SOCIAL GOSPEL AND LIFE AFTER DEATH

Since at death we emigrate from the social life of mankind, the future life of the individual might seem to lie outside the scope of our discussion. But in truth our conceptions of the life hereafter are deeply affected by the fundamental convictions of the social gospel.

There is no inherent contradiction whatever between the hope of the progressive development of mankind toward the Kingdom of God and the hope of the consummation of our personal life in an existence after death. The religious belief in the future life is often bitterly attacked by social radicals because in actual practice the deep interest in it, which is cultivated by the Church, weakens interest in social justice and acts as a narcotic to numb the sense of wrong. The more the social gospel does its work within the Church, the more will this moral suspicion against the doctrine of the future life lessen.

Belief in future life is not essential to religious faith. The religious minds who speak to us from the pages of the Old Testament, though they probably believed in future existence, apparently gained neither comfort nor incentive from that belief. There is doubtless an increasing number of religious men and women today who find their satisfaction in serving God now, but expect their personal existence to end at death.

The hope that we shall survive death is not a self-evident proposition. When it is intelligent it is an act of faith—a tremendous assertion of faith. It may get support from science, from philosophy, or from psychical research, but its main supports are the resurrection of Christ, his teachings, and the common faith of the Christian Church, which all embolden the individual. Further, the sense of personality, which is intensified and ennobled by the Christian life, rises to the sense of imperishable worth in the assurance that we are children of God.

The hope of a higher life for the race does not solve the problem of the individual. It is a matter of profound satisfaction to those whose life has really matured and been effective to think that they have made a contribution to the richness and the redemption of the race. But none of us lives out his life fully. There are endowments in us which have never been put to use for others, and tastes and cravings which have been starved and suppressed. Moreover, only a small percentage of men and women under present conditions are able to develop their powers beyond the feeblest beginnings. A large percentage die in childhood; uncounted others have been used up by labor—shrunken and intimidated souls. Where do they come in? Is it enough for them to think that they have been laid like sills in the mud that future generations may live in the mansion erected on their dead bodies and souls? Besides, the best society on earth cannot last forever. This planet may end at any time and it is sure to die by collision or old age some time. What then will be the net product of all our labors? Plainly a man has a larger and completer hope if he looks forward to eternal life for himself as well as to a better destiny for the race.

It is our business, however, to Christianize both expectations. It is possible to fear hell and desire heaven in a pagan spirit, with a narrow-minded selfishness that cares nothing for others, and is simply an extension to the future life of the grabbing spirit fostered by the kingdom of evil. The desire for heaven gets Christian dignity and quality only when it arises on the basis of that solidaristic state of mind which is cultivated by the social gospel.

Two theories, quite unlike, are held as private opinions by many Christian individuals, though not sanctioned by traditional theology. The theory of conditional immortality is largely based on evolutionary ideas. It holds that only those will survive who have attained to a spiritual life capable of surviving. The theory of reincarnation, which has been held by a few eminent minds in theology and by many outside of it, comes to us mostly through theosophical channels from the East. It teaches that we live in a succession of lives, each of them adapted to the spiritual attainments of the individual and disciplinary in its effect; through them we can gradually exhaust the possibilities of human life and rise to spiritual levels above man.

Both theories, however, are somewhat aristocratic in their effect. When we consider the terrible inequality of opportunity for spiritual development in our present world, it does not convey a sense of Christian solidarity to think of a minority climbing into eternal life while the majority wilt away like unfertilized blossoms.

The most unattractive element in the orthodox outlook on the future life is the immediate fixity of the two states. When we die, our destiny is immediately and irrevocably settled for us. . . . The idea of a fixed condition is so unlike any life we know and so contradictory of our aspiration that our imagination stands still before a tedious sameness of bliss. The rich diversification in Dante shows the possibility of the other view. We want the possibility of growth. We cannot conceive of finite existence or of human happiness except in terms of growth. It would be more satisfactory for modern minds and for Christian minds to think of an unlimited scale of ascent toward God, reaching from the lowest to the highest, within which every spirit would hold the place for which it was fitted, and each could advance as it grew. This would satisfy our sense of justice. Believers in the social gospel will probably agree that some people have deserved hell and ought to get theirs. But no man, in any human sense of justice, has deserved an eternity of hell. On the other hand, it jars our sense of justice to see some individuals go to heaven totally exempt. They have given hell to others and ought to have a taste of it somewhere, even if they are regenerate and saved men.

This idea would also satisfy our Christian faith in the redeeming mercy of God. In this ascending scale of beings none would be so high that he could not be drawn still closer to God, and none so low that he would be beyond the love of God. God would still be teaching and saving all. If we learned in heaven that a minority were in hell, we should look at God to see what he was going to do about it; and if he did nothing, we should look at Jesus to see how this harmonized with what he taught us about his Father; and if he did nothing, something would die out of heaven. . . . The conception of a permanent hell was tolerable only while God was conceived as an autocratic sovereign dealing with his subjects; it becomes intolerable when the Father deals with his children.

Today many Protestants are allowing the physical fires of hell to go out, and make the pain of hell to consist in the separation from God. They base the continuance of hell not on the sovereign decree of God but on the progressive power of sin which gradually extinguishes all love of good and therewith all capacity for salvation. But this remains to be proven. Who has ever seen a man that had no soft spot of tenderness, no homesick yearning after uprightness left in him?

The idea of the two fixed groups does not satisfy any real requirement. Men justly feared the earlier Universalist doctrine that all men enter salvation at death. That took sin lightly and offended the sense of justice. The idea of a scale of life in which each would be as far from God and in as much darkness and narrowness as he deserved would constitute a grave admonition to every soul. Indeed it would contain more summons to self-discipline than the present idea that as long as a man is saved at all, he is saved completely and escapes all consequences. Today the belief in hell has weakened in great numbers of people, and in that case there is no element of fear at all to aid men in self-control. The Christian idea would have to combine the just effects of sin for all and the operation of saving mercy on all.

Our personal eschatology is characterized by an unsocial individualism. In the present life we are bound up with wife and children, with friends and workmates, in a warm organism of complex life. When we die, we join—what? a throng of souls, an unorganized crowd of saints, all carrying harps but not even organized into an orchestra? The question is even debated whether we shall know each other in heaven, and whether we shall remember and have a sense of identity. What satisfaction would there be in talking to Isaiah or Paul if they could not remember what books they wrote and at last set our minds at rest on those questions of criticism? Anyone trained in the mind of Christ by the social gospel wants organic relations of duty and friendship. How can we become more Christlike on earth or in heaven except by love and service? The chief effort of the Holy Spirit in our earthly life was to develop our capacity for love and our sense of solidarity and responsibility. Is this training to go for nothing in heaven, or is this present life the real preparation for the kind of life we are to live there, and the basis for promotion and growth? If the future life is to be the consummation of all that is good and divine here, it must offer fellowship with God and man. This is the point to be insisted on in our popular teaching, and not the painlessness and the eternal rest.

And how about labor and service? Is not our heaven too much a heaven of idleness? It looks as if it has been conceived by oppressed and exploited people who regarded labor as a curse and wanted a rest more than anything else. The social gospel wants to see all men on earth at productive work, but none doing too much of it. It carries that expectation into the idea of heaven.

The social gospel would add the kindred fact that a large proportion of individuals are left so underdeveloped by our earthly social system that they deserve a heavenly postgraduate course to make it up to them. It would be a great joy in heaven to find men trooping in from mines and shops, and women from restaurant kitchens and steaming laundries, and getting their long delayed college education.

This suggests another form of service. We are all conscious of having failed in some of our human relations, giving indifference instead of sympathy, idleness instead of service, laying our burdens on others without lending a hand with theirs. Some have done little in the sum total of their life except to add to the weight on others, and monopolizing the opportunities which ought to have been shared by many. The future life offers a chance for reparation, not by way of kindness but of justice. Suppose that a stockholder has taken large dividends out of a mill-town, leaving only the bare minimum to the workers, and stripping their lives of what could humanize them. He followed the custom of his day, and the point of view of his social class hid the injustice from his conscience. But in the other world he sees things differently and becomes a belated convert to the social gospel. About him are the men and women whose souls he has starved. Would not justice demand that he remain on the lower levels of life with them until he was able to take upward with him all whom he had retarded? Suppose that a man sent a child into life without accepting the duties of fatherhood, breaking the spirit of a girl and her family, and leaving his child to be submerged in poverty and vice. Would it not be just and Christian to require that he serve the soul of his child until it is what it might have been? Such labor and expiation might well keep us busy for some part of eternity, and in doing it, relationships of love and service would be formed which would make us fit to live closer to the source of love.

LIFE IN GOD IS IMMORTAL

Of course some of the ideas I have ventured to put down are simply the play of personal fancy about a fascinating subject. There are only a few things which we can claim with any assurance, and these are not based on a single prediction, or on some passage, the origin or meaning of which may be disputed, but on the substance of the gospel of Christ. These are: that the love of God will go out forever to his children, and especially to the neediest, drawing them to him and, where necessary, saving them; that personality energized by God is ever growing; that the law of love and solidarity will be even more effective in heaven than on earth; and that salvation, growth, and solidarity are conditioned on interchange of service.

The worth of personality, freedom, growth, love, solidarity, service—these are marks of the Kingdom of God. In Christ's thought the Kingdom of God was to come from heaven to earth, so that God's will would be done on earth as it is in heaven. So, then, it exists in heaven; it is to be created on earth. All true joys on earth come from partial realizations of the Kingdom of God; the joy that awaits us will consist in living within the full realization of the Kingdom. Our labor for the Kingdom here will be our preparation for our participation hereafter. The degree in which we have absorbed the laws of the Kingdom into our character will determine our qualification for the life of heaven. If in any respect we have not been saved from the kingdom of evil, we shall be aliens and beginners in the Kingdom of God. Thus heaven and earth are to be parts of the same realm. Spiritual influences come to us; spiritual personalities go out from us. When our life is in God it has continuity.

8

The Special Task of the Church

THE CHURCH ITSELF NOT FREE OF EVIL

The higher the institution, the worse it is when it goes wrong. The most disastrous backsliding in history was the deterioration of the Church. Long before the Reformation the condition of the Church had become the most serious social question of the age. It weighed on all good men. The Church, which was founded on democracy and brotherhood, had, in its higher levels, become an organization controlled by the upper classes for parasitic ends, a religious duplicate of the coercive State, and a chief check on the advance of democracy and brotherhood. Its duty was to bring love, unity, and freedom to mankind; instead, it created division, fomented hatred, and stifled intellectual and social liberty. It is proof of the high valuation men put on the Church that its corruption seems to have weighed more heavily on the conscience of Christendom than the corresponding corruption of the State. At least the religious revolution antedated the political revolution by several centuries. Today the Church is practically free from graft and exploitation; its sins are mainly sins of omission; yet the contrast between the idea of the Church and its reality, between the force for good which it might exert and the force which it does exert in public life, produces profounder feelings than the shortcomings of the State.

WHERE THE CHURCH IS WEAK

When we consider the ideas prevalent in the churches, their personnel, and their sources of income, has the Church a message of repentance and an evangel for this modern world?

Let us sum up. The powerlessness of the old evangelism is only the most striking and painful demonstration of the general state of the churches. Its cause is not local nor temporary. It does not lie in lack of hard work or of prayer or of keen anxiety. It lies in the fact that modern life has gone through immense changes and the Church has not kept pace with it in developing the latent moral and spiritual resources of the gospel which are needed by the new life. It has most slighted that part of the gospel which our times most need. It lacks an ethical imperative which can induce repentance. In private life its standard differs little from respectability. In commerce and industry, where the unsolved and painful problems lie, it has no clear message, and often claims to be under no obligation to have one. In the State churches the State has dominated; in the free churches the capitalist class dominates. Both influences are worldly—in favor of things as they are and against the ideals which animate the common people. The people are becoming daily more sensitive to the class cleavage of society. The Church suffers under the general resentment against the class with which it is largely identified. To this must be added the fact that the spirit of free inquiry engineered by modern science neutralizes the dogmatic authority with which the Church has been accustomed to speak.

TRUE VERSUS FALSE PROPHETS

Our prophetic books contain constant reference to the "false prophets." These were not the preachers of an idolatrous religion, but men who claimed to deliver the word of Jehovah. Neither were they always conscious liars. They were the mouthpiece of the average popular opinion, and they drew their inspiration from the self-satisfied patriotism which seemed so very identical with trust in Jehovah and his sanctuary. They were apparently the great majority of the prophetic order; the prophets of our Bible were the exceptional men. The false prophets corresponded to those modern preachers who act as eulogists of existing conditions, not because they desire to deceive the people, but because they are really so charmed with things as they are and have never had a vision from God to shake their illusion. The logic of events proved to be on the side of these great Hebrews who asserted that black is really black, even if you call it white, and that a wall built with untempered mortar and built out of plumb is likely to topple. Because history backed their predictions, they are now in the Bible and revered and inspired.

It is well to note, however, that the prophets took no vindictive pleasure in prophesying evil, as some modern prophets enjoy beating the broom of God's vengeance about the ears of the people. While Jeremiah was foretelling the destruction of Jerusalem, his heart was breaking. It is significant that as soon as the disaster had come, the tone of prophecy changed. As long as the people were falsely optimistic, the prophets opposed their false hopelessness. On the ruins of the temple Jeremiah foretold its restoration, the return of the people, and a new era for his desolated country. As soon as the news of the destruction of the temple reached Ezekiel in exile, his threats changed to comfort and promises. This was not instability; it was loyalty to facts and hostility to illusions. Because they believed in the immutability of the moral law, they had to tremble at any departure from it, but they could also feel its unshaken strength under their feet when all things went to pieces about them. These pessimists were really profoundly and magnificently optimistic. They never doubted the ultimate victory of Jehovah, of his righteousness and of his people. The time may come in our own country when the smiling optimists will be the most frightened and helpless of all, and when the present pessimists will be the only ones who have any hopes to cheer and any clear convictions to guide.

The great prophets whom we revere were not those whom their own age regarded most. They were the men of the opposition and of the radical minority. They probably had more influence over posterity than over their own generation. Their attacks on existing conditions brought dangerous attacks upon them in return. A later day can always study with complacency the attacks made on the vested interests in a previous epoch, and the championship of eternal principles always seems divine to a generation that is not hurt by them. Jesus summed up the impression left on him by Old Testament history by saying that prophets have no honor in their own country and in their own generation. It is always posterity which builds their sepulchres and garnishes their tombs.

A CALL TO THE NEW EVANGELISM

The new evangelism which shall . . . again exert the full power of the gospel cannot be made to order nor devised by a single man. It will be the slow product of the fearless thought of many honest men. It will have to retain all that was true and good in the old synthesis, but advance the human conception of salvation one stage closer to the divine conception. It will have to present a conception of God, of life, of duty, of destiny, to which the best religious life of our age will bow. It will have to give an adequate definition of how a Christian man should live under modern conditions, and then summon men to live so.

A compelling evangel for the working class will be wrought out only by men who love that class, share its life, understand the ideals for which it is groping, penetrate those ideals with the religious spirit of Christianity, and then proclaim a message in which the working people will find their highest self. They will never be reached by a middle-class gospel preached down at them with the consciousness of superiority.

If we personally are to have a share in working out the new evangel, we shall have to open to two influences and allow them to form a vital union in our personalities. We must open our minds to the spirit of Jesus in its primitive, uncorrupted, and still unexhausted power. That spirit is the fountain of youth for the Church. As a human organization it grows old and decrepit like every other human organism. But again and again it has been rejuvenated by a new baptism in that spirit. We must also keep our vision clear to the life of our time. Our age is as sublime as any in the past. It has a right to its own appropriation and understanding of the gospel. By the decay of the old, God himself is forcing us on to seek the new and higher.

This attempt at a diagnosis of our ills is not offered in a spirit of condemnation, but of personal repentance and heart-searching. We all bear our share of guilt. I have full faith in the future of the Christian Church. A new season of power will come when we have put our sin from us. Our bitter need will drive us to repentance. The prophetic spirit will awaken among us. The tongue of fire will descend on twentieth-century men and give them great faith, joy, and boldness, and then we shall hear the new evangel, and it will be the old gospel.

TO REDEEM SOCIETY IS THE CHURCH'S TASK

The chief purpose of the Christian Church in the past has been the salvation of individuals. But the most pressing task of the present is not individualistic. Our business is to make over an antiquated and immoral economic system; to get rid of laws, customs, maxims, and philosophies inherited from an evil and despotic past; to create just and brotherly relations between great groups and classes of society; and thus to lay a social foundation on which modern men individually can live and work in a fashion that will not outrage all the better elements in them. Our inherited Christian faith dealt with individuals; our present task deals with society.

The Christian Church in the past has taught us to do our work with our eyes fixed on another world and a life to come. But the business before us is concerned with refashioning this present world, making this earth clean and sweet and habitable.

The purpose of all that Jesus said and did and hoped to do was always the social redemption of the entire life of the human race on earth. If we regard him in any sense as our leader and master, we cannot treat as secondary what to him was the essence of his mission. If we regard him as the Son of God, the revelation of the very mind and evil and nature of the Eternal, the obligation to complete what he began comes upon us with an absolute claim to obedience.

Life is the sacred spark of God in us, and the best of our race have reverenced it most. Wherever life is held precious, and restored and redeemed when broken or soiled, there is God's country, and there the law of Christ prevails.

THE SAVING POWER OF THE CHURCH

The saving power of the Church does not rest on its institutional character, on its continuity, its ordination, its ministry, or its doctrine. It rests on the presence of the Kingdom of God within her. The Church grows old; the Kingdom is ever young. The Church is a perpetuation of the past; the Kingdom is the power of the coming age. Unless the Church is vitalized by the ever nascent forces of the Kingdom within her, she deadens instead of begetting.

THE FUNCTION OF EVANGELISM

There are two kinds of evangelization. The one proclaims new truth, as Jesus did to his nation, or Paul to the Gentiles, or as a missionary does to the heathen. The other summons men to live and act according to the truth which the Church has previously instilled into their minds and which they have long accepted as true. The latter is, on the whole, the kind which we have to do. To be effective, evangelism must appeal to motives which powerfully seize men, and it must hold up a moral standard so high above their actual lives that it will smite them with conviction of sin. If the motives urged seem untrue, or remote, or if the standard of life to which they are summoned is practically that on which they are living, the evangelistic call will have little power. The two questions which every Christian worker should investigate for himself are these: Are the traditional motives still effective? And is the moral standard held up by the Church such as to induce repentance?

THE RESPONSIBLE MINISTRY

The ministry, in particular, must apply the teaching functions of the pulpit to the pressing questions of public morality. It must collectively learn not to speak without adequate information; not to charge individuals with guilt in which all society shares; not to be partial, and yet to be on the side of the lost; not to yield to political partisanship, but to deal with moral questions before they become political issues and with those questions of public welfare which never do become political issues. They must lift the social questions to a religious level by faith and spiritual insight. The larger the number of ministers who attempt these untrodden ways, the safer and saner will those be who follow. By interpreting one social class to the other, they can create a disposition to make concessions and help in securing a peaceful settlement of social issues.

THE MAIN DUTY OF CHRISTIANS

These fundamental utterances of the mind of Christ are the supreme law of Christendom. Anything that contradicts them is anarchic. The chief business of

Christian men today is to translate them into terms large enough to make them fully applicable to modern social life. Our economic organization will have to be transformed in these directions. It is unchristian as long as men are made inferior to things, and are drained and used up to make profit. It will be Christian when all industry is consciously organized to give to all the maximum opportunity of a strong and normal life. It is unchristian when it systematizes antagonism, inequality, tyranny, and exploitation. It will be Christian when it is organized to furnish the material foundation for love and solidarity by knitting men together through common aims and united work, by making their relations just and free, and by making the material welfare of each dependent on the efficiency, moral vigor, and good will of all.

JESUS' CHALLENGE TO THE CHURCH

The platform for ethical progress laid down in the Sermon on the Mount is a great platform. When Tolstoi first realized the social significance of these simple sentences, it acted as a revelation which changed his life. Even men who reject the supernatural claims of Christianity uncover before the Sermon on the Mount. Yet its fate is tragic. It has not been "damned with faint praise," but made ineffective by universal praise. Its commandments are lifted so high that nobody feels under obligations to act on them. Only small sections of the Christian Church have taken the sayings on oaths, nonresistance, and love of enemies to mean what they say and to be obligatory. Yet all feel that the line of ethical and social advance must lie in the direction traced by Jesus, and if society could only climb out of the present pit of predatory selfishness and meanness to that level, it would be heaven.

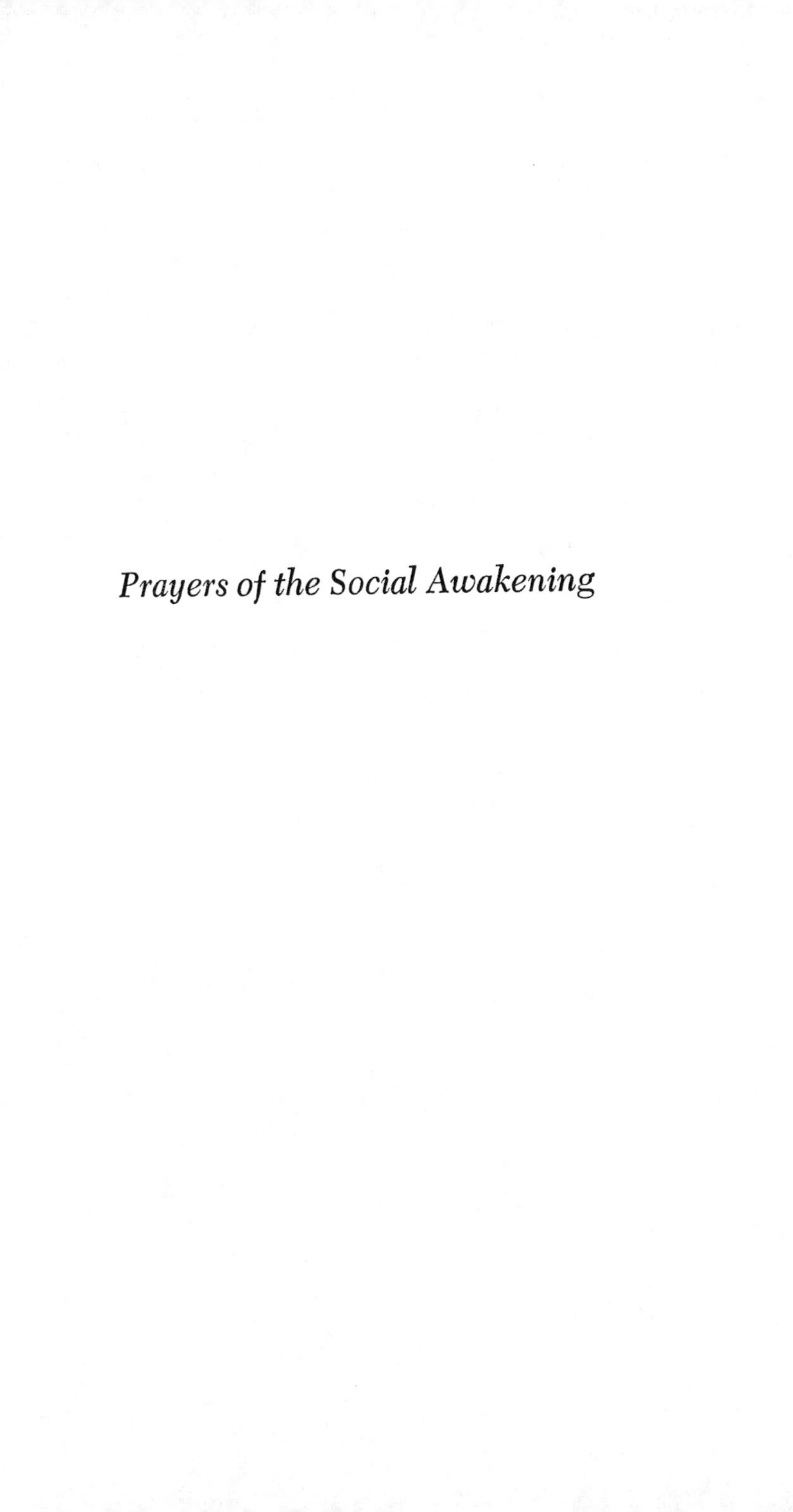

Prayers of the Social Awakening

❧ 9 ❧

Prayers of the Social Awakening

THE SOCIAL MEANING OF THE LORD'S PRAYER

The Lord's Prayer is recognized as the purest expression of the mind of Jesus. It crystallizes his thoughts. It conveys the atmosphere of his childlike trust in the Father. It gives proof of the transparent clearness and peace of his soul.

It first took shape as a protest against the wordy flattery with which men tried to wheedle their gods. He demanded simplicity and sincerity in all expressions of religion, and offered this as an example of the straightforwardness with which men might deal with their Father. Hence the brevity and conciseness of it:

In praying use not vain repetitions, as the Gentiles do: for they think that they shall be heard for their much speaking. Be not therefore like unto them: for your Father knoweth what things ye have need of before ye ask him. After this manner therefore pray ye:

> Our Father who art in heaven,
> Hallowed be thy name.
> Thy kingdom come.
> Thy will be done, as in heaven, so on earth.
> Give us this day our daily bread.
> And forgive us our debts, as we also have forgiven our debtors.
> And bring us not into temptation, but deliver us from the evil one.—Matt. 6:7-13 (American Revision)

The Lord's Prayer is so familiar to us that few have stopped to understand it. The general tragedy of misunderstanding which has followed Jesus throughout the centuries has frustrated the purpose of his model prayer also. He gave it to stop vain repetitions, and it has been turned into a contrivance for incessant repetition.

The churches have employed it for their ecclesiastical ritual. Yet it is not ecclesiastical. There is no hint in it of the Church, the ministry, the doctrines of theology, or the sacraments—though the Latin Vulgate has turned the petition for the daily bread into a prayer for the "super-substantial bread" of the sacrament.

It has also been used for the devotions of the personal religious life. It is, indeed, profoundly personal. But its deepest significance for the individual is revealed only when he dedicates his personality to the vaster purposes of the Kingdom of God, and approaches all his personal problems from that point of view. Then he enters both into the real meaning of the Lord's Prayer, and into the spirit of the Lord himself.

The Lord's Prayer is part of the heritage of social Christianity which has been appropriated by men who have had little sympathy with its social spirit. It belongs to the equipment of the soldiers of the Kingdom of God. I wish to claim it here as the great charter of all social prayers.

When he bade us say "Our Father," Jesus spoke from that consciousness of human solidarity which was a matter of course in all his thinking. He compels us to clasp hands in spirit with all our brothers and thus to approach the Father together. This rules out all selfish isolation in religion. Before God no man stands alone. Before the All-seeing he is surrounded by the spiritual throng of all to whom he stands related near and far, all whom he loves or hates, whom he serves or oppresses, whom he wrongs or saves. We are one with our fellowmen in all our needs. We are one in our sin and our salvation. To recognize that oneness is the first step toward praying the Lord's Prayer aright. That recognition is also the foundation of social Christianity.

The three petitions with which the prayer begins express the great desire which was fundamental in the heart and mind of Jesus: "Hallowed be thy name. Thy kingdom come. Thy will be done, as in heaven, so on earth." Together they express his yearning faith in the possibility of a reign of God on earth in which his name shall be hallowed and his will be done. They look forward to the ultimate perfection of the common life of humanity on this earth, and pray for the divine revolution which is to bring that about.

There is no request here that we be saved from earthliness and go to heaven which has been the great object of churchly religion. We pray here that heaven may be duplicated on earth through the moral and spiritual transformation of humanity, both in its personal units and its corporate life. No form of religion has ever interpreted this prayer aright which did not have a loving understanding for the plain daily relations of men, and a living faith in their possible spiritual nobility.

And no man has outgrown the crude selfishness of religious immaturity who has not followed Jesus in setting this desire for the social salvation of mankind ahead of all personal desires. The desire for the Kingdom of God precedes and outranks everything else in religion, and forms the tacit presupposition of all our wishes for ourselves. In fact, no one has a clear right to ask for bread for his body or strength for his soul, unless he has identified his will with this all-embracing purpose of God, and intends to use the vitality of body and soul in the attainment of that end.

With that understanding we can say that the remaining petitions deal with personal needs.

Among these the prayer for the daily bread takes first place. Jesus was never as "spiritual" as some of his later followers. He never forgot or belittled the elemental need of men for bread. The fundamental place which he gives to this petition is a recognition of the economic basis of life.

But he lets us pray only for the bread that is needful, and for that only when it becomes needful. The conception of what is needful will expand as human life develops. But this prayer can never be used to cover luxuries that debilitate, nor accumulations of property that can never be used but are sure to curse the soul of the holder with the diverse diseases of mammonism.

In this petition, too, Jesus compels us to stand together. We have to ask in common for our daily bread. We sit at the common table in God's great house, and the supply of each depends on the security of all. The more society is socialized, the clearer does that fact become, and the more just and humane its organization becomes, the more will that recognition be at the bottom of all our institutions. As we stand thus in common, looking up to God for our bread, every one of us ought to feel the sin and shame of it if he habitually takes more than his fair share and leaves others hungry that he may surfeit. It is inhuman, irreligious, and indecent.

The remaining petitions deal with the spiritual needs. Looking backward, we see that our lives have been full of sin and failure, and we realize the need of forgiveness. Looking forward, we tremble at the temptations that await us and pray for deliverance from evil.

In these prayers for the inner life, where the soul seems to confront God alone, we should expect to find only individualistic religion. But even here the social note sounds clearly.

This prayer will not permit us to ask for God's forgiveness without making us affirm that we have forgiven our brothers and are on a basis of brotherly love with all men: "Forgive us our debts, as we also have forgiven our debtors." We shall have to be socially right if we want to be religiously right. Jesus will not suffer us to be pious toward God and merciless toward men.

In the prayer, "Lead us not into temptation," we feel the human trembling of fear. Experience has taught us our frailty. Every man can see certain contingencies just a step ahead of him and knows that his moral capacity for resistance would collapse hopelessly if he were placed in these situations. Therefore Jesus gives voice to our inarticulate plea to God not to bring us into such situations.

But such situations are created largely by the social life about us. If the society in which we move is rank with sexual looseness, or full of the suggestiveness and solicitations of alcoholism; if our business life is such that we have to lie and cheat and be cruel in order to live and prosper; if our political organization offers an ambitious man the alternative of betraying the public good or of being thwarted and crippled in all his efforts, then the temptations are created in which men go under, and society frustrates the prayer we utter to God. No church can interpret this petition intelligently which closes its mind to the debasing or invigorating influence of the spiritual environment furnished by society. No man can utter this petition without conscious or unconscious hypocrisy who is helping to create the temptations in which others are sure to fall.

The words, "Deliver us from the evil one," have in

them the ring of battle. They bring to mind the incessant grapple between God and the permanent and malignant powers of evil in humanity. To the men of the first century that meant Satan and his host of evil spirits who ruled in the oppressive, extortionate, and idolatrous powers of Rome. Today the original spirit of that prayer will probably be best understood by those who are pitted against the terrible powers of organized covetousness and institutionalized oppression.

Thus the Lord's Prayer is the great prayer of social Christianity. It is charged with what we call "social consciousness." It assumes the social solidarity of men as a matter of course. It recognizes the social basis of all moral and religious life even in the most intimate personal relations to God.

It is not the property of those whose chief religious aim is to pass through an evil world in safety, leaving the world's evil unshaken. Its dominating thought is the moral and religious transformation of mankind in all its social relations. It was left us by Jesus, the great initiator of the Christian revolution; and it is the rightful property of those who follow his banner in the conquest of the world.

✠

FOR THE FATHERHOOD OF GOD

O thou great Father of us all, we rejoice that at last we know thee. All our soul within us is glad because we need no longer cringe before thee as slaves of holy fear, seeking to appease thine anger by sacrifice and self-inflicted pain, but may come like little children, trustful and happy, to the God of love. Thou art the only true Father, and all the tender beauty of our human loves is the reflected radiance of thy loving kindness, like the moonlight from the sunlight, and testifies to the eternal passion that kindled it.

Grant us growth of spiritual vision, that with the passing years we may enter into the fullness of this our faith. Since thou art our Father, we may not hide our sins from thee, but overcome them by the stern comfort of thy presence. By this knowledge uphold us in our sorrows and make us patient even amid the unsolved mysteries of the years. Reveal to us the larger goodness and love that speak through the unbending laws of thy world. Through this faith make us the willing equals of all thy other children.

As thou art ever pouring out thy life in sacrificial father-love, may we accept the eternal law of the cross and give ourselves to thee and to all men. We praise thee for Jesus Christ, whose life has revealed to us this faith and law, and we rejoice that he has become the first-born among many brethren. Grant that in us, too, the faith in thy fatherhood may shine through all our life with such persuasive beauty that some who still creep in the dusk of fear may stand erect as free sons of God, and that others who now through unbelief are living as orphans in an empty world may stretch out their hands to the great Father of their spirits and find thee near.

FOR THIS WORLD

O God, we thank thee for this universe, our great home; for its vastness and its riches, and for the manifoldness of the life which teems upon it and of which we are part. We praise thee for the arching sky and the blessed winds, for the driving clouds and the constellations on high. We praise thee for the salt sea and the running water, for the everlasting hills, for the trees, and for the grass under our feet. We thank thee for our senses by which we can see the splendor of the morning, and hear the jubilant songs of love, and smell the breath of the springtime. Grant us, we pray thee, a heart wide open to all this joy and beauty, and save our souls from being so steeped in care or so darkened by passion that we pass heedless and unseeing when even the thorn-bush by the wayside is aflame with the glory of God.

Enlarge within us the sense of fellowship with all the living things, our little brothers, to whom thou hast given this earth as their home in common with us. We remember with shame that in the past we have exercised the high dominion of man with ruthless cruelty, so that the voice of the Earth, which should have gone up to thee in song, has been a groan of travail. May we realize that they live, not for us alone, but for themselves and for thee, and that they love the sweetness of life even as we, and serve thee in their place better than we in ours.

When our use of this world is over and we make room for others, may we not leave anything ravished by our greed or spoiled by our ignorance, but may we hand on our common heritage fairer and sweeter through our use of it, undiminished in fertility and joy, that so our bodies may return in peace to the great mother who nourished them and our spirits may round the circle of a perfect life in thee.

FOR THE KINGDOM OF GOD

O Christ, thou hast bidden us pray for the coming of thy Father's kingdom, in which his righteous will shall be done on earth. We have treasured thy words, but we have forgotten their meaning, and thy great hope has grown dim in thy Church. We bless thee for the inspired souls of all ages who saw afar the shining City of God, and by faith left the profit of the present to follow their vision. We rejoice that today the hope of these lonely hearts is becoming the clear faith of millions. Help us, O Lord, in the courage of faith to seize what has now come so near, that the glad day of God may dawn at last. As we have mastered Nature that we might gain wealth, help us now to master the social relations of mankind that we may gain justice and a world of brothers. For what shall it profit our nation if it gain numbers and riches, and lose the sense of the living God and the joy of human brotherhood?

Make us determined to live by truth and not by lies, to found our common life on the eternal foundations of righteousness and love, and no longer to prop the tottering house of wrong by legalized cruelty and force. Help us to make the welfare of all the supreme law of our land, that so our commonwealth may be built strong and secure on the love of all its citizens. Cast down the throne of Mammon who ever grinds the life of men, and set up thy throne, O Christ, for thou didst die that men might live. Show thy erring children at last the way from the City of Destruction to the City of Love, and fulfill the longings of the prophets of humanity. Our Master, once more we make thy faith our prayer: "Thy kingdom come! Thy will be done on earth!"

✠

A SOCIAL LITANY

From the sins that divide us, from all class bitterness and race hatred, from forgetfulness of thee and indifference to our fellow-men:

Good Lord, deliver us.

From the corruption of the franchise and of civil government, from greed and from the arbitrary love of power:

Good Lord, deliver us.

From the fear of unemployment and the evils of overwork, from the curse of child-labor and the ill-paid toil of women:

Good Lord, deliver us.

From the luxury that enervates, from the poverty that stultifies:

Good Lord, deliver us.

That it may please thee to unite the inhabitants of every city, state, and nation in the bonds of peace and concord:

We beseech thee to hear us, Good Lord.

That thy followers may be strong to achieve industrial justice, and to bid the oppressed go free:

We beseech thee to hear us, Good Lord.

That the labor movement may be confirmed in disinterested honor, and that the employers of labor may fashion their dealings according to the laws of equity:

We beseech thee to hear us, Good Lord.

That thou wilt help us to give all men health of body and soul:

We beseech thee to hear us, Good Lord.

That the watchword of the Christian State, "Thou shalt love thy neighbor as thyself," may become a command with power:

We beseech thee to hear us, Good Lord.

That the spirit of reconciliation may be made manifest among men:

We beseech thee to hear us, Good Lord.

That it may please thee to inspire thy Church with the vision of the New Jerusalem coming down from heaven to men, and that thy Kingdom may come on earth:

We beseech thee to hear us, Good Lord.

The grace of our Lord Jesus Christ, and the love of God, and the fellowship of the Holy Spirit be with us all evermore.

AMEN.

✠

FOR THOSE WHO COME AFTER US

O God, we pray thee for those who come after us, for our children, and the children of our friends, and for all the young lives that are marching up from the gates of birth, pure and eager, with the morning sunshine on their faces. We remember with a pang that these will live in the world we are making for them. We are wasting the resources of the earth in our headlong greed, and they will suffer want. We are building sunless houses and joyless cities for our profit, and they must dwell therein. We are making the burden heavy and the pace of work pitiless, and they will fall wan and sobbing by the wayside. We are poisoning the air of our land by our lies and our uncleanness, and they will breathe it.

O God, thou knowest how we have cried out in

agony when the sins of our fathers have been visited upon us, and how we have struggled vainly against the inexorable fate that coursed in our blood or bound us in a prison-house of life. Save us from maiming the innocent ones who come after us by the added cruelty of our sins. Help us to break the ancient force of evil by a holy and steadfast will and to endow our children with purer blood and nobler thoughts. Grant us grace to leave the earth fairer than we found it; to build upon it cities of God in which the cry of needless pain shall cease; and to put the yoke of Christ upon our business life that it may serve and not destroy. Lift the veil of the future and show us the generation to come as it will be if blighted by our guilt, that our lust may be cooled and we may walk in the fear of the Eternal. Grant us a vision of the far-off years as they may be if redeemed by the sons of God, that we may take heart and do battle for thy children and ours.

ON THE HARM WE HAVE DONE

Our Father, we look back on the years that are gone, and shame and sorrow come upon us, for the harm we have done to others rises up in our memory to accuse us. Some we have seared with the fire of our lust, and some we have scorched by the heat of our anger. In some we helped to quench the glow of young ideals by our selfish pride and craft, and in some we have nipped the opening bloom of faith by the frost of our unbelief.

We might have followed thy blessed footsteps, O Christ, binding up the bruised hearts of our brothers and guiding the wayward passions of the young to firmer manhood. Instead, there are poor hearts now broken and darkened because they encountered us on the way, and some perhaps remember us only as the beginning of their misery or sin.

O God, we know that all our prayers can never bring back the past, and no tears can wash out the red marks with which we have scarred some life that stands before our memory with accusing eyes. Grant that at least a humble and pure life may grow out of our late contrition, that in the brief days still left to us we may comfort and heal where we have scorned and crushed. Change us by the power of thy saving grace from sources of evil into forces for good, that with all our strength we may fight the wrongs we have aided, and aid the right we have clogged. Grant us this boon, that for every harm we have done, we may do some brave act of salvation, and that for every soul that has stumbled or fallen through us, we may bring to thee some other weak or despairing one, whose strength has been renewed by our love, that so the face of thy Christ may smile upon us and the light within us may shine undimmed.

FOR THE PROPHETS AND PIONEERS

We praise thee, Almighty God, for thine elect, the prophets and martyrs of humanity, who gave their thoughts and prayers and agonies for the truth of God and the freedom of the people. We praise thee that amid loneliness and the contempt of men, in poverty and imprisonment, when they were condemned by the laws of the mighty and buffeted on the scaffold, thou didst uphold them by thy spirit in loyalty to thy holy cause.

Our hearts burn within us as we follow the bleeding feet of thy Christ down the centuries, and count the mounts of anguish on which he was crucified anew in his prophets and the true apostles of his spirit. Help us to forgive those who did it, for some truly thought they were serving thee when they suppressed thy light, but O, save us from the same mistake! Grant us an unerring instinct for what is right and true, and a swift sympathy to divine those who truly love and serve the people. Suffer us not by thoughtless condemnation or selfish opposition to weaken the arm and chill the spirit of those who strive for the redemption of mankind. May we never bring upon us the blood of all the righteous by renewing the spirit of those who persecuted them in the past. Grant us rather that we, too, may be counted in the chosen band of those who have given their life as a ransom for the many. Send us forth with the pathfinders of humanity to lead thy people another day's march toward the land of promise.

And if we, too, must suffer loss, and drink of the bitter pool of misunderstanding and scorn, uphold us by thy Spirit in steadfastness and joy because we are found worthy to share in the work and the reward of Jesus and all the saints.

FOR A SHARE IN THE WORK OF REDEMPTION

O God, thou great Redeemer of mankind, our hearts are tender in the thought of thee, for in all the afflictions of our race thou hast been afflicted, and in the sufferings of thy people it was thy body that was crucified. Thou hast been wounded by our transgressions and bruised by our iniquities, and all our sins are laid at last on thee. Amid the groaning of creation we behold thy spirit in travail till the sons of God shall be born in freedom and holiness.

We pray thee, O Lord, for the graces of a pure and holy life that we may no longer add to the dark weight of the world's sin that is laid upon thee, but may share with thee in thy redemptive work. As we have thirsted with evil passions to the destruction of men, do thou fill us now with hunger and thirst for justice that we may bear glad tidings to the poor and set at liberty all who are in the prison-house of want and sin. Lay thy spirit upon us and inspire us with a passion of Christ-like love that we may join our lives to the weak and oppressed and may strengthen their cause by bearing their sorrows. And if the evil that is threatened turns to smite us and if we must learn the dark malignity of sinful power, comfort us by the thought that thus we are bearing in our body the marks of Jesus, and that only those who share in his free sacrifice shall feel the plenitude of thy life. Help us in patience to carry forward the eternal cross of thy Christ, counting it joy if we, too, are sown as grains of wheat in the furrows of the world, for only by the agony of the righteous comes redemption.

FOR THE CO-OPERATIVE COMMONWEALTH

O God, we praise thee for the dream of the golden city of peace and righteousness which has ever haunted the prophets of humanity, and we rejoice with joy unspeakable that at last the people have conquered the freedom and knowledge and power which may avail to turn into reality the vision that so long has beckoned in vain.

Speed now the day when the plains and the hills and the wealth thereof shall be the people's own, and thy freemen shall not live as tenants of men on the earth which thou hast given to all; when no babe shall be born without its equal birthright in the riches and knowledge wrought out by the labor of the ages; and when the mighty engines of industry shall throb with a gladder music because the men who ply these great tools shall be their owners and masters.

Bring to an end, O Lord, the inhumanity of the present, in which all men are ridden by the pale fear of want while the nation of which they are citizens sits throned amid the wealth of their making; when the manhood in some is cowed by helplessness, while the soul of others is surfeited and sick with power which no frail son of the dust should wield.

O God, save us, for our nation is at strife with its own soul and is sinning against the light which thou aforetime has kindled in it. Thou hast called our people to freedom, but we are withholding from men their share in the common heritage without which freedom becomes a hollow name. Thy Christ has kindled in us the passion for brotherhood, but the social life we have built denies and slays brotherhood.

We pray thee to revive in us the hardy spirit of our forefathers that we may establish and complete their work, building on the basis of their democracy the firm edifice of a co-operative commonwealth, in which both government and industry shall be of the people, by the people, and for the people. May we, who now live, see the oncoming of the great day of God, when all men shall stand side by side in equal worth and real freedom, all toiling and all reaping, masters of nature but brothers of men, exultant in the tide of the common life, and jubilant in the adoration of thee, the source of their blessings and the Father of all.

Index of Topics and Sources

1. The Christian Gospel and Our Social Crisis

2. The Kingdom of God

The Doctrine of the Kingdom Is the Theology for the Social Gospel
A Theology for the Social Gospel, pp. 139-143
Democratizing God
A Theology for the Social Gospel, pp. 174-175, 186-187
Democratizing the Holy Spirit
A Theology for the Social Gospel, pp. 188-189
The Kingdom of God as Love and Labor
A Theology for the Social Gospel, pp. 54-55
The Kingdom Comes by Slow Growth
The Social Principles of Jesus, pp. 88-89

3. THE SOCIAL PRINCIPLES OF JESUS

All Are Children of God
The Social Principles of Jesus, pp. 9, 13-14, 22-24
Each Person Is Valuable
Christianizing the Social Order, p. 327
We Belong Together
Christianizing the Social Order, pp. 327-328
Solidarity of Family and Nation
The Social Principles of Jesus, p. 24
Equality the Foundation of Political Democracy
Christianity and the Social Crisis, pp. 247-249
Christianizing the Social Order, p. 300
The Consciousness of Humanity Must Be Achieved
The Social Principles of Jesus, pp. 27-28, 33, 38-39
Jesus Trusted and Loved the "Common People"
The Social Principles of Jesus, pp. 39-40
The Hebrew Prophets and the "Common People"
The Social Principles of Jesus, pp. 41-42
There Are None Beneath His Care
The Social Principles of Jesus, p. 2

A Theology for the Social Gospel, p. 57
The Truth in the Doctrine of Original Sin
A Theology for the Social Gospel, pp. 57-58
The Biological Aspects of Original Sin
A Theology for the Social Gospel, pp. 58-59
Defects in the Doctrine of Original Sin
A Theology for the Social Gospel, p. 59
The Social Heredity of Sin
A Theology for the Social Gospel, pp. 59-62
The Source of Authority in Sin
A Theology for the Social Gospel, pp. 62-63, 66
The Social Transmission of Sin
A Theology for the Social Gospel, pp. 67-68, 71-72
The Evil That Men Do Lives After Them
A Theology for the Social Gospel, pp. 78-80
False Conceptions of the Kingdom of Evil
A Theology for the Social Gospel, pp. 83-85
The Passing of Belief in Evil Spirits
A Theology for the Social Gospel, p. 86
The Power and Reality of Evil Remain
A Theology for the Social Gospel, p. 87
The Sin of All Is in Each
A Theology for the Social Gospel, pp. 90-92

5. Salvation: Personal and Social

6. Religion and Social Reform

9. Prayers of the Social Awakening